Praise for
Your Time to Rise

"In *Your Time to Rise*, Arivee encourages all women of color to break free from outdated expectations and claim the life they deserve. With a mix of sass and wisdom, Arivee shares her own journey and delivers no-nonsense tools to help you ditch the limits and create a life on your terms."

—**Giovanna González,** best-selling author of *Cultura & Cash*

"*Your Time to Rise* is an essential read for any woman navigating the complexities of societal expectations, particularly within the Latino community. This book offers profound insight into how cultural norms influence our choices and gently guides readers through a transformative journey of self-discovery. By helping us develop awareness, trust our inner voice, and ask the universe for what we truly desire, it empowers us to break free from the pressures of being the perfect mom, wife, or employee. Ultimately, this book is a road map to aligning with our soul's purpose and living authentically and fully."

—**Yvonne Castañeda,** LICSW, professor and author of the critically acclaimed *Pork Belly Tacos with a Side of Anxiety*

"*Your Time to Rise* is a must-read for all high-achieving women of color. Arivee's four-part framework makes living a fulfilling and joyful life much more accessible and realistic. You'll see yourself in these pages, and it will change your life!"

—Alaina Fingal, CEO and founder of The Organized Money

"In recent years, our fundamental relationship with work has changed. We no longer are relegated to asking what we can get. We are now empowered to ask for what we want. And if the latter is too daunting, *Your Time to Rise* gives you a blueprint to finding your truest and most authentic answer. In this book, that's part guide and part pep talk, Arivee provides holistic frameworks to navigate transitions. With every page, you feel her challenging you to explore new levels while simultaneously cheering you on. While so many other books provide formulas, Arivee creates the space for you to customize both the experience and the outcome. Arivee's personal story of being a first-generation Latina is one that resonates deeply with me and gives me more agency to shine even brighter because of the path she has already forged ahead. If you're ready to unleash your power within, and change the trajectory of generations to come, this book is for you!"

—Aundrea Cline-Thomas, host of *The NEXT Best Thing* podcast

YOUR TIME TO
RISE

ARIVEE VARGAS

YOUR TIME TO RISE

UNLEARN LIMITING BELIEFS,

UNLOCK YOUR POWER,

AND UNLEASH YOUR TRUEST SELF

GREENLEAF
BOOK GROUP PRESS

Published by Greenleaf Book Group Press
Austin, Texas
www.gbgpress.com

Distributed by Greenleaf Book Group

For ordering information or special discounts for bulk purchases, please contact Greenleaf Book Group at PO Box 91869, Austin, TX 78709, 512.891.6100.

Design and composition by Greenleaf Book Group
Cover design by Greenleaf Book Group

Publisher's Cataloging-in-Publication data is available.

Print ISBN: 979-8-88645-265-5

eBook ISBN: 979-8-88645-266-2

To offset the number of trees consumed in the printing of our books, Greenleaf donates a portion of the proceeds from each printing to the Arbor Day Foundation. Greenleaf Book Group has replaced over 50,000 trees since 2007.

Printed in the United States of America on acid-free paper

25 26 27 28 29 30 31 32   10 9 8 7 6 5 4 3 2 1

First Edition

To my children Julian, Maya, and Thali:

*May you always have the courage to live a life
that is the truest reflection of who you are.*

The best thing about your life
is that it is in a constant
state of design.
This means you have, at all times,
the power to redesign it.
Make moves, allow shifts,
smile more, do more, do less,
say no, say yes.
Just remember,
when it comes to your life,
you are not just the artist,
but the masterpiece as well.
—Cleo Wade

CONTENTS

AUTHOR'S NOTE

According to most statistics, as the daughter of Dominican immigrant parents, I shouldn't have even graduated high school, much less gone to college, attended law school, practiced at large law firms, or anything else I've done. Like you, I've worked my behind off for professional success. There were blessings and burdens I carried along that journey, partly related to the messages I'd internalized throughout my life of what it meant to be "good," to "sacrifice," to "just be grateful," to "keep your head down and do the work," to "keep it moving," to "be strong," and to continue to prove your value.

The identity crisis that arose within me after the birth of my first child forced me to figure out who I was and what I truly wanted—without the weight of everything I had been carrying and the titles I had worked so hard to earn. With each career pivot and life transition I've had since then, I've had to learn how to shed identities to make way for new ones and to continue to shed beliefs that didn't serve me anymore, all to make room for those that did. For almost ten years, I've engaged in this work and coached others to do the same.

What I've learned is this: If you want to feel better about your life and live fully, you must anchor yourself in your truest truth, envision what you want in the future, and go in that direction. It takes unmasking yourself and being intentional about aligning what's on the inside with what you're doing on the outside.

Being a mother adds layers of complexities and challenges to this. As of this writing, I'm the mother of three children ages nine and under. As I was accelerating in my career and having kids, I experienced burnout, panic attacks, anxiety, depression, and the baby blues. As women, too often we sacrifice ourselves and aim for perfectionist-type standards in every area of our lives, and this way of living is causing us too much suffering. It causes too much internal conflict, and the mental load can be too heavy to bear. So many of us have lost the joy in living. And we deserve to feel fulfillment and joy.

But this book isn't just for moms. If you're at any type of inflection point or crossroads in your life or career, this book is for you. I'm on a mission to show women—especially women of color and first-generation women doing the motherhood and career thing—how to live with more fulfillment and joy. After I finished the final draft of this book, I left a job I loved to pursue that mission full-time. The calling became too strong to ignore, and I had to answer the call. It was my most significant inflection point yet, and I'm thankful that this book will have reached your hands almost one full year after I turned the final page on the previous chapter of my life and began this new one.

In this book, I walk you through a 4-Part Framework to take you from stuck, confused, or uncertain, to clear and confident on your path forward to finding joy and fulfillment in your life. I pull from my experiences as a first-generation Latina, a mother, a former Big Law lawyer and Human Resources leader in Leadership Development, and a certified High-Performance coach for high-achieving women of color and first-generation women. To maintain confidentiality, I have altered the names of my clients and changed details to protect their identities and stories.

While I refer to research studies that highlight the experiences of women of color, the experiences of women of color are not monolithic. When I speak specifically about my Latina experience, I don't speak for all Latinas. Even within our cultures and communities, we have a wide range of experiences, resources, and histories. There is rich diversity among all our experiences, as well as commonalities.

As you read on, I hope you see yourself in these pages and that you recognize how much power you have right now to make the changes to *your* life that you're longing to make, or to finally make the decision you've been grappling with. I hope you see yourself as the greatest catalyst there could ever be. Thank you for picking up this book and for being open to exploring what fulfillment and joy can look like for you. You deserve it.

—Arivee Vargas

PART 1

GAIN CLARITY

Knees on the Floor

"Shame never tells the truth. It tells you
you are not enough. The truth is you are. It tells you
you have to be perfect. The truth is you don't."

—Cleo Wade

Racing at full speed, my heart was about to burst out of my chest. I gasped for air, as my hands and knees hit the hardwood floor. With tears streaming down my face and nearly out of breath, I cried to my husband. He had walked into our bedroom seconds earlier. Between heavy breaths, I said to him: "I can't do this anymore. I can't."

I could feel my husband looking down at me. I didn't look up at him. I couldn't.

He bent toward me, took my hands in his, one at a time, and helped me off the floor. He walked me a few steps to the edge of our bed, and we both sat down.

He said, "I can see this is hard for you. What do you need?"

I still couldn't look at him. My eyes stayed focused on the floor. My neck and shirt were wet from tears, no matter how hard I tried to wipe them away.

This is not how I am supposed to feel, I thought. Isn't being a new mom supposed to be some blissful experience, where you finally meet the baby you've been waiting to welcome to the world for so long? I felt shame that I wasn't grateful for simply having a baby. I was embarrassed of my tears and my obvious inability to keep it together.

This isn't me, I thought. What is happening? I'm not someone whose husband finds her on the floor crying when he gets home from work. I'm not even someone who cries like that. I'm a first-generation Latina. I'm a lawyer and a fighter. I've been through a lot, and I'm tough.

WHERE I'M COMING FROM

I come from a long line of strong women who toughed it out. They got it done. They birthed their children without epidurals (my mother had nearly all eleven pounds of me without one). They worked full-time jobs, did drop off and pick up at school, daycare, and after-school programs. They had dinner on the table by 5:30 p.m. sharp, gave us baths, put us to bed, made sure we had the right size clothes for the appropriate seasons, and all the other things that mothers do. And they never complained.

Not once did I see or hear my mother, or any other woman in my big Dominican family, express any problem with being a new mother or a working mom. They never even said that parenting was difficult or that they were having a hard time! They loved hard, laughed hard, and disciplined us hard (although sometimes they have selective amnesia on that last one. Sorry, it's true!). I always attributed the stress and tension I felt as a young child to the fact that we didn't have a lot of money (for living in the States), and my parents worked full-time. They had my sister and me at the tender ages of twenty-one and twenty-four, when my father was working more than one job and in school to get his college degree. I cannot imagine the weight of their responsibilities.

Despite life's stressors, my parents created so many joyful moments during my sister's and my childhood. I remember so vividly being woken up around 4 a.m. when I was little to get in the car and drive to Florida. Back then, you didn't have to wear a seatbelt and my sister and I were small enough to lie down in the back seat. My family loves the beach, so that's where we were headed. Regardless of where we stayed, if we had each other and the beach and a pool, we were happy. One time, we stayed at a Sheraton, and I was floored at how fancy it was; I'm sure my jaw must have dropped. We ate dinner at a small Cuban restaurant with some of the best rice, black beans, and platanos I've ever had. On our way out of the restaurant, there was a glass case with gum and candy for sale, and my parents always got us a five-stick pack of Big Red. To me, those days were perfect, including when we went to Myrtle Beach, except when my sister got sun poisoning and we all had to go to the ER. That probably wasn't too fun for her.

As a young girl, my weekends were spent with tíos, tías, cousins, my mom, and my sister dancing in our living room to Madonna, Janet Jackson, Juan Luis Guerra, Jerry Rivera, Fernandito Villalona,

Michael Jackson, the Jets, Menudo, and any other cross-section of salsa, merengue, bachata on the one hand and American pop, R&B, and hip-hop on the other. Think Madonna's "La Isla Bonita" or "Papa Don't Preach" with "Ojala Que Llueva Café" by Juan Luis Guerra. In middle school, my sister and I fell into Mariah Carey, TLC, Mary J. Blige, Salt-N-Pepa, and who can forget Tevin Campbell and Boyz II Men?

We had so much fun dancing and lip-syncing using brushes and kitchen utensils for microphones. I often fell down from spinning so fast during my dance moves and trying to look into the camera my mom was holding. She always recorded us (with an old-school VHS video camera) and sent the tapes to family back in the Dominican Republic, so they could see how we were doing and how much we were growing. You can imagine me losing my balance more than once or twice. I'd hit the rug on the floor and disappear from the frame, then you'd see my head pop back up. The show must go on, right! This was true even when my sister and I launched into our dance moves, and she fell teeth first into the brown wooden coffee table in our living room. She chipped her tooth; I sustained no injuries. We didn't have a ton of space to move around, but we made the most of what we had.

My mother was present, and she didn't lose her patience that easily. If she had a hard time, she didn't show it. My aunts were the same way, and they were doing the same things as my mom, working and raising kids in their early twenties. These are strong women. They did (and still) live life with so much love and humor.

There were plenty of comments on appearance as a child. "Tu vas a salir con tu pelo asi?" ("You're going to leave with your hair like that?") or "Ponte pintalabio" ("Put on your lipstick."). It was mostly about what others would think of how we presented ourselves, because presentation was important. My mother always made us wear these itchy ass tights with dresses for special occasions. There was an emphasis on appearance and of doing things to ensure people wouldn't have a reason to gossip or say anything negative. Most of our positive affirmations came in the form of a constant barrage of kisses, hugs, and laughter. If there is one thing I know for sure, it's that my family was never lacking in the expression of love and affection.

The very act of providing for us was a monumental testament to our parents' love: food (La Bandera—the Dominican spin on rice, beans, and meat), clothing (think Bradlees, Marshalls, and Jordan Marsh), and a house to live in. Our home when I was young was not in a safe area, but my parents managed that by not letting us go past our driveway. We couldn't walk down the street by ourselves, and we definitely could not go to the bodega down the street. My parents' priority was to keep us safe, and they did everything in their power to protect us.

One of the huge sacrifices they made for us was to pay for Catholic school, which they thought would provide the best education. It was not cheap and was about twenty minutes away from where we lived. My sister and I were the only two Latinas in our K-8 school and remained two of several students of color for eight whole years.

In third grade, some boy called me a "spic," and it was the first time I heard a racial slur directed at me. I remember how he said it, when he said it, and the way he was sitting at his desk when he said it. He said it as if it was no big deal. I didn't respond because I was in shock. My mother talked to the teacher that same day, but nothing happened to that kid. Nothing. I still had to deal with him for the next five years.

The thing is, I was so concerned with trying to fit in with my White peers; I didn't know how to be both Dominican and American. I was born in the United States, but I was constantly juggling two identities and felt forced to choose one. I was too gringa (American) for Dominicans and too Dominican for Americans.

> I was constantly juggling two identities and felt forced to choose one.

My children live in a very different world. They're learning about and celebrating diverse cultures from the jump, due largely to where we have the opportunity to live. From infancy, their friends have been from a wide range of racial and ethnic backgrounds, but that's not how I grew up. You were either White or other, and you weren't "allowed" to be in both lanes or in between them, either. There was much less acceptance of difference back then. Forget about any celebration of it.

There was slightly more racial and ethnic diversity in high school (but not much). Two years ahead of me, my sister went to a mostly White public high school with strong academic standing through the school choice program. It was about thirty minutes north of where we lived. When it was time for me to go to high school, going to school where we lived wasn't an option. My parents sold our house, and we moved into the district where my sister's high school was located so I could go there, too.

I graduated in the top three of my eighth-grade class, but the Catholic school education my parents worked so hard to pay for led to some challenges for me. When I took the freshman placement exams, we discovered I was two years behind in math. In English class, when the teacher returned our first papers of the semester, mine said, "Writing tutor" across the top; it wasn't even good enough to merit a grade. I studied and eventually tested into the math class for my grade level and ability, but it was a tough start to high school. Later, when I got into college, I had a classmate question (to my face) how I could have been accepted to Boston College. It felt like people were always asking me to justify my place.

Despite the responsibilities of keeping my sister and me safe, paying for our education and the mortgage, feeding us, putting clothes on our backs, while making sure we had fun, my mother kept it together. My aunts did, too.

Why then, with only one baby, couldn't I?

COMING UNDONE

My experience as a new mother was not even close to what I thought it was going to be. For starters, I can count on one hand the number of times my then four-month-old son slept more than four hours in a row. Because he didn't sleep, I didn't sleep. I was nursing him, but because he wasn't growing at the rate appropriate for an infant, I had to supplement with formula. That I couldn't nourish him with my breast milk was an unspoken source of shame for me. I know, we always say, "If breastfeeding doesn't work, and you have to use formula, do it. Don't stress. It's not worth it." And though, logically,

I understood that, I didn't believe it. My thoughts kept churning in my mind that there was something wrong with me, and I was a bad mother because I couldn't feed my baby with my body. I wanted so desperately to suck up the sleep deprivation and push down how I was feeling, but I couldn't.

My husband went back to work a few weeks after the baby was born, and I was home by myself. My son was born in early March, so the days were still short. When the sun started to go down at 5 p.m., so did my mood. I felt pure dread as night fell and cried when it started getting dark outside because I knew what was coming: a baby who didn't sleep. When I'd nestled with him in those too damn expensive "swivel" chairs from Pottery Barn and rocked him in my arms, it appeared he was asleep. But as soon as I started to stand up, his one eye would open and look at me, saying, "I'm still awake! Ha! Ha!" Let me tell you, no fancy chair is going to help your baby fall asleep. You'd be good with an old wooden one.

It wasn't just me. My sister drove over every night, after a full day of working as a pediatrician. She tried all her tricks to get my son to fall and stay asleep during the transfer from the rocking chair to the crib. She stayed with him in his room until 11 p.m. with the pacifier, rocking him the way the books tell you to, and he did the same thing to her: open one eye and fuss. Ultimately, we gave up and let him sleep in our arms. All of us. Even my sister. She'd walk out of the room, hand the baby to us, and say, "I tried."

IDENTITY CRISIS

The physical strain on my body, my guilty feelings about being a bad mother, and the shame around my inability to be grateful for the experience of motherhood was compounded by the sense that I was losing my identity as a person. I often thought, "Is this all I am now? Am I just a mother?" I didn't want to "just be a mother." I was my own person before I got married and had children.

The "me" before is part of the reason I didn't take my husband's last name when I got married at thirty years old. I'm a Vargas. Vargas is my father's family name. I'm Dominican. I'm proud of my roots, my community, and my people, and I couldn't bear the idea of letting the Vargas name go. On the low, my husband still complains about me not taking his name, but he also knows why I can't, and deep down, he respects that. I mean, you'd probably have to ask him.

On our wedding day, I had a few minutes of meltdown when I was about to walk down the aisle with my father. The bridal party and my future husband were already at the altar. The only two still standing at the back of the church were my father and me. As we began the journey, I abruptly stopped and squeezed my dad's arm. He said, "Take your time. We go when you're ready." I had a full-on crying moment. Not pretty tears, either. It hit me that I was about to commit to sharing my life with someone. To step into marriage, you feel like you may be leaving a piece of you behind, and that's what I was mourning: the part of me I thought I had to leave behind. That part of me was the piece that always wanted freedom to do what I wanted, when I wanted. And I desperately didn't want to lose myself in my marriage. That didn't happen, but I was scared it might. Well, terrified is probably a more accurate description. Hence, the waterfall of tears.

Two years later when our son was born, it felt like I was losing myself in motherhood instead. There was something deeper stirring, beyond the physical and emotional exhaustion I felt as a new mother. I had lost my footing. There was nothing keeping me on the ground. No anchor and no compass. I had the baby blues, which culminated in the moment my hands and knees hit the floor, along with my entire world.

> I had lost my footing. There was nothing keeping me on the ground.

As exhausted as I was, I wanted to go back to work when my son was three months old—not because I had clients that needed me or because my work was fulfilling—but because work had been my life since I was twelve. Not as an attorney, obviously, but at my after-school jobs and with my schoolwork. Work was where I derived a sense of accomplishment and achievement, where I felt valuable. The better I performed, the better I felt about myself.

I didn't separate Arivee the person from Arivee the lawyer. For me, they were one and the same. For me, it wasn't even about the substance of the work; it was about how I felt validated through my work and how my work (and work ethic) was praised by other people. At law firms, doing excellent work is the baseline. But junior associates are recognized for going above and beyond, for answering emails late at night, on weekends and over holidays, and volunteering to be staffed on cases over the holidays. That's what made you great versus good. It was about how far you were willing to go to show your loyalty, work ethic, and commitment, which led, of course, to overworking and sacrificing time with family and friends. There were too many 2 a.m. nights to count. I equated my work performance and productivity with my value as a person, and when I was no longer working, my source for validation was gone, too. That's how I started my legal career, and I carried that mindset and belief into both of my federal clerkships and the second law firm I joined after that.

By the time I went back to work after having my son, I knew I couldn't keep up the same pace as before, and I wanted more out of my career and my life; I knew I was meant for more. Deep inside, I knew I was playing small. But I didn't want to face or accept that truth. I was physically and emotionally exhausted, struggling with my identity as a new mother, and if all of that wasn't hard enough, I was battling the thought that I didn't want the very job that shaped my professional identity.

Let's Be Honest . . .

- What were the people who raised you like?
- What memories do you carry with you from childhood?
- Have you ever struggled to maintain your identity after becoming a mother, or after a significant transition or change?
- What life events have brought you to a "knees on the floor" moment?

The Weight of Expectations

"Imagine how much happier we would be,
how much freer to be our true individual selves,
if we didn't have the weight of . . . expectations."

—Chimamanda Ngozi Adichie

Let's go back, way back in time. (No, not like the Blackstreet song "Don't Leave Me." Such a great '90s song, though.)

THE GRIND: CULTURAL AND FAMILIAL PROGRAMMING

Growing up, I received the message that if I wanted to be successful, I would need to work very hard and make a lot of sacrifices, and it wasn't going to be easy. Now, to be clear, I believe success in any form requires work, discipline, focus, and perseverance. However, the core of the message I received was if I wanted to be successful, it was going to be a grind, and it would always be a grind. The grind is the requirement for success. If there is no grind, there is no success. And so, I always pursued whatever was in front of me with the grind in mind. I believed it was supposed to be hard, and I was supposed to sacrifice myself in the process.

Because of the expectation to work hard and push through, many professional women of color and mothers struggle to prioritize our self-care and well-being because it was not role modeled for us. Rest was seen as unproductive or lazy, primarily because our parents worked so hard to provide for us; they didn't have the privilege of rest. They were always on the go and moving from one task to the next whether it was cooking, cleaning, organizing, fixing the house, or working. So, if you were resting, you weren't working inside or outside the home. There was always a bill to pay, and money didn't come easily. Our parents weren't investing anything in the stock market back then. The possibility of losing money—money they had earned with their blood, sweat, and tears—was simply not a viable option.

Our parents were often in survival mode. They had to push through all the challenges, including discrimination, and be strong to put a roof over our heads on a daily basis. They were private about their struggles, worries, and fears. They didn't want to let us see or know how hard it was for them. As a parent now, I understand and respect that. As a child though, you feel energy in a room. You sense the energy of stress and worry from your parents, even if it's unspoken. And you learn that expressing worries and fears is not something that's okay to do. You don't want to make it harder on them. You don't know if there will be space for your worries; they're already dealing with so much. You learn to stuff it down, to "forget about it," and to keep it moving. These were coping skills.

Of course, as my sister and I got older, I felt my parents were less and less in that survival space. We moved to a different house in the same city, and my father moved into roles that compensated him better than the ones he had before. I could write an entire book on each of my parents; their stories are inspirational and powerful, but their stories aren't mine to tell. (I already asked, ha!) But I want to make it clear that I come from a place of privilege when it comes to how much my parents have given me. My father helped me complete financial aid applications to college. He was the one who told me to apply to Boston College (and I was aghast, because I had no intention of staying in Boston for college). When I was accepted to BC, I was given a strong financial aid package. NYU was a no-go; my parents made it clear neither they nor I could afford it. I'd be strapped with so much debt; it didn't make sense. My parents were right there to help me through that entire process and tell me some hard truths about college debt.

In college, I hustled to limit how much money we'd have to spend on tuition. To keep costs down, I had a work-study job in the library, became a resident assistant, and won a prestigious scholarship in honor of Archbishop Óscar A. Romero, one of my personal heroes. And after all of that, I still had about $17,000 in college debt. The day of my graduation, my parents handed me a piece of paper showing they had paid my debt off. I graduated from college debt-free because of them and their sacrifices. My parents knew my sister and I would continue to work hard for our dreams in law school (me) and medical school (my sister); they didn't raise women who settle. But they also knew exactly how it feels to carry a heavy load, so they gave my sister and I the gift of a lighter one.

As I achieved milestones I'd only ever dreamed of, I continued to receive messages from the world around me that I needed to work harder (on top of my grind), and that "more" was better. The environments I navigated from law school (i.e., "when you're not studying, other people are") into my first law firm ("you're only as good as your last assignment") reinforced these messages. To be clear, those statements are factually accurate. It's what I made those statements mean that was problematic. I always felt the pressure to prove myself: to prove I was smart enough to be in the spaces I occupied. I thought, I may not be as smart as these other people, but I can outwork them all. Hard work is in my DNA. I'm a Vargas. Look out.

Early in my legal career, I don't remember ever feeling like I "belonged." Having White colleagues you enjoy working with is not the same as feeling like you belong in a space completely. There weren't many lawyers who looked like me, and the ones who did became and remain my closest friends and mentors. I wasn't just fighting to prove myself for me, but for my entire Latinx community. I felt the need to represent my community to the larger, White, older male population that dominates large law firms: the old guard typical of corporate America. And being one of the very few Latinas made me visible. I recognized that visibility as both a burden and an opportunity to show that WE (not just me) are smart enough and WE deserve to be in these spaces. Had there been more representation, even in partnership ranks, I may not have felt so compelled to represent for my community, but I didn't want to ruin it for other Latinas coming after me. This is unique to women of color in workplaces where they are underrepresented. It's something we carry with us, wherever we go.

A TRIPLE WHAMMY

As first-generation professional women of color, the weight of expectations on our shoulders is heavy. When we add motherhood to the equation, it's a triple whammy: woman, woman of color, and mother. Often our own communities and cultures teach us that we must and can do it all, and be all things to all people, even at our own expense. We carry this weight of expectations every day.

The Good Mom

Let's talk about childcare and household responsibilities, which traditionally (and continually) fall to women. Decades of research have shown that women take on significantly more responsibility for housework and childcare than men. For example, women of color, especially those with childcare responsibilities, were more likely to leave the workforce during the COVID-19 pandemic.[1] Like all working mothers, mothers of color face significant challenges when attempting to integrate work and family responsibilities. However, these challenges are compounded by the cultural expectations around motherhood and caregiving that are more prominent in communities of color. For example,

Latina mothers are 1.6 times more likely than White mothers to be responsible for all childcare and housework, and Black mothers are twice as likely to be handling these duties for their families.[2]

Women of color experience cultural pressure to conform to traditional gender roles and family structures, which often makes ripe a situation where they feel they must choose between being a good mother and advancing their careers. In other words, the weight of expectations becomes so difficult, many working mothers of color no longer believe they can experience the healthy integration of career and family.

There is no shortage of studies to illustrate this reality.

- The *Gender and Society* journal found that Black, Latina, and Asian-American mothers experience cultural expectations around intensive mothering, which can lead to high levels of work-family conflict.

- The *Journal of Marriage and Family* found that Black and Latina mothers experience greater levels of work-family conflict than White mothers, which was attributed in part to cultural expectations that mothers should prioritize their families over their careers.

- Studies have found that cultural values and norms around motherhood and family obligations can contribute to greater work-family conflict and associated stress for Black, Latina, and Asian-American mothers.[3]

Statistics aside, the perception and expectation is that a "good" mom bakes fresh cookies for the bake sale at her child's school;

volunteers in their classroom; attends all the school events (because nothing could be more important than that); drives her children to all their activities; runs a tight ship at home with homework time, bedtime, wake up time; cooks whole food dinners (because nothing is more important than having a freshly cooked meal, and what mother would want their family to be unhealthy); doesn't lose her patience with her children or yell at them; always has the house—especially the kitchen—clean at all times; organizes play dates; takes her children to their friends' birthday parties; makes sure they are dressed nicely each day with a fresh pair of clothes (God forbid your child wants to wear the same sweatshirt they wore the day before); and ensures their child's hair is "presentable" (because to have your child's hair looking "messy" is a reflection of how much you don't care as a mother). Oh, and I forgot about *planning* birthday parties. Your child's birthday party, especially when they are younger, must have a theme, so figure out how many weeks you need to have everything in advance from Etsy or Amazon. I'm not saying you do all or any of these things; it's the expectations of what it means to be a "good mom" that can weigh on us.

The Good Wife

In many households, including Latinx homes, "*El hombre es quien manda*" ("The man is in charge."). There's a reason our mothers always told us to ask our fathers for permission to do things. Women have a voice, but it's not quite as powerful as the man's. This is not by coincidence. Latinas, specifically, have been programmed and socialized to remain submissive and play small. Most of the Latinas I know including family and friends are anything but passive and submissive, let me tell you. But we've all had to go against the grain of how we've been socially conditioned.

Researchers have identified specific cultural messages of expectations reinforced in the Latinx community that Latinas must unlearn. One is "*marianismo*," which emphasizes the role of women as family and home centered; it encourages passivity and self-sacrifice.[4] As children, Latinas received messages that women are the nurturers and are to demonstrate respect for patriarchal values. Simpatico research found that women avoid conflicts to maintain harmony, and they self-silence at their personal expense.

On top of that, we all know, the "good" wife is always looking fly at home and finds time to work out. She never eats her kids' leftovers or processed snacks, and she doesn't "let herself go" just because she has kids. A good wife cooks for her partner, especially her man, because the way to a man's heart is through his stomach. She has to look and interact with her partner the way she did before all the responsibilities with her children and career kicked in. (Can you picture my eyes rolling?)

God forbid, she comes home from work and changes into comfortable clothes, especially sweatpants. She has to look "put together" and she has to at least have some makeup on, because her face and hair say a lot about how much she loves and cares about herself (the eye roll is getting more intense now).

And let's address the elephant in the room: a good wife has sex with her male partner, preferably at least three times or more a week. No excuses about headaches or being tired are allowed, because her partner needs to be satisfied. Her needs aren't paramount in that moment. Besides, if she doesn't have sex, he may just go find it elsewhere. Her job is to keep the fires going and keep the relationship fresh. That's on her.

Objectively, it sounds ridiculous. But you and I both feel the pressure to live up to one, a few, or many of these unrealistic expectations. I'm exhausted simply listing them, and we haven't even discussed our professional lives yet!

The Good Employee

The pressure to be a "perfect" mother and wife is compounded by how we are expected to behave and present ourselves at work. A "good" employee is committed, loyal, reliable, and responsive. She says yes to any and all additional projects, even if they do not provide her with visibility or the opportunity for advancement. She repeatedly goes above and beyond. She works hard, often to the point of exhaustion to "get it done." She sacrifices time with herself, her friends, and her family for the good of those she works for and with. She is trained to be a "good" team player and to be "nice." She is trained to wait her turn, to listen, and to flex her style to those around her.

After all, her parents sacrificed so much for her to be in this professional position, and she feels the need to make good on that sacrifice. She feels the need to show her family and colleagues and her community (because she represents them) that she can do this and so she performs at the highest level. She knows all eyes are on her. Or, at least, that's how it feels. She achieves and achieves, and it feels like it will never be enough.

OUR OWN EXPECTATIONS

As much as we want, on some level, to nail the triple whammy—be the good mom, the good wife, and the good employee—here's the kicker: "Good" is not good enough for us.

All the women of color I have met and worked with over the years have very high expectations of themselves. In fact, *no one's* expectations are higher than the ones we have of ourselves; they're higher even than those put upon us by our workplaces, families, communities, and society at large. For us, if we are high achieving in one area, we want to be high achievers in *all areas*: as mothers, daughters, wives or partners, leaders at work, in our communities, and with our self-care.

> *No one's* expectations are higher than the ones we have of ourselves.

The do-it-all, be-it-all mindset is killing our ability to recognize and appreciate all that we do, let alone celebrate it. And it's killing our well-being—we simply cannot do everything at such a high level all at the same time. We cannot do everything *at any level* all at the same time.

Yes, the physical activity of working and taking care of our families is tiring, but the mental and emotional gymnastics we endure takes an exhausting toll. Constantly switching our attention from one part of our lives to the other and making decisions each day about our personal, home, and work life in a constant cycle is unsustainable. It's not even humanly possible. Our bodies, minds, and spirits need rest.

Nevertheless, because of the nonstop be-it-all and do-it-all we expect of ourselves, when we cannot achieve it (because no one can), we feel guilty and mentally beat ourselves up. We tell ourselves we should be able to handle it; we should be able to do better; we should suck it up and never complain. Because our mothers and our *tías* never did, and they had it even harder than we do!

Before we go any further, I'd like to make a pact with you though. Can we agree that blaming our culture, communities, or families for the messages we received and may have internalized growing up is not going to serve us and help us on our journeys to living the lives we want and deserve? While a new level of awareness and acknowledging their impact is helpful, blaming them is not. Our parents did the best with the tools they had. If they could have rested, they would have. If they could have taken care of themselves more, they would have. If they knew how intensely the cultural messages and behavioral "norms" impacted their children, they may have done things differently. It's unreasonable to fully expect our parents to have intervened for every possible message we would end up internalizing to our detriment. They made decisions and took actions that reflected what was role modeled for them.

We can take a moment to remember they also role modeled critical life lessons and values that have made us badass powerhouses: tenacity, adaptability, perseverance, and the ability to drive toward results, and let's not forget the value of family and community. Let's lean into those and be proud of them and give our parents plenty of grace. One day, we might be asking our children for the same grace we need to afford our parents. Let's lean into accepting and embracing that we're carving our own path, because there is no blueprint for us to follow on how we integrate work, family, community, self-love, and self-care to live the life we want.

Let's Be Honest . . .

- What were the messages you received when you were growing up? What did those messages mean to you then?
- How do those messages manifest in your life? How do they affect how you navigate work and the other areas of your life?
- Do any of the cultural expectations I experienced ring true for you, too?

Just the Way It Is: Workplace Realities

"I am not lucky. You know what I am? I am smart,
I am talented, I take advantage of the opportunities
that come my way and I work really, really hard.
Don't call me lucky. Call me a badass."

—Shonda Rhimes

A t an annual women of color lawyer conference years ago, I was struck by a remark during one of the panels. A top law firm partner said, "If you ask why you have to be the 'one' to make partner, navigate the work-life challenges that come with the title, and the expectation of being constantly available, the answer is you do. There aren't many who look like us in these spaces, so yes, we have to be the ones to do it. That's just the way it is."

It was the last line that got me. "That's just the way it is" sounded like we don't have a choice. We simply have to accept our plight? Is there not another way?

Sitting in the audience, all I felt was sorrow—sorrow that even if we didn't necessarily want to become partner or general counsel, we had to suck it up and do it anyway. Because if we don't, who will? We know women, and especially professional women of color, are significantly underrepresented in leadership roles in corporate America. According to McKinsey & Company's Women in the Workplace 2023 report, "Women of color face the steepest drop-off in representation from entry-level to C-suite positions. As they move up the pipeline, their representation drops by two-thirds." While women represent about 25 percent of C-suite leaders, women of color represent 6.25 percent.[1] And here was an added pressure: the expectation from our own community of high-achieving women of color to bear the brunt of traditional trailblazing.

Through no fault of our own, our choices are limited. We operate within systems and structures that were not created for women, women of color, or mothers who work outside the home. In fact, the systems and structures we operate within are designed to keep us out. We receive conflicting messages on every level: cultural, social, familial, professional, and personal. These conflicted messages are both external and internal, and the obstacles those messages create are very real.

Where, when, and how did we come up with the belief that our lot in life is "just the way it is"? When did we come to accept powerlessness and lack of choice as a way of life?

What are we even doing to ourselves?

ONE OF THE FEW

In most professional business settings, we often have the burden and blessing of being one of the few. It's a blessing because we have been afforded opportunities our ancestors, family, and community could have only dreamed of. We have a chance to "make it" and create a better future for those coming after us. We have the opportunity to role model how to be successful—the way we uniquely define success—for others.

On the other hand, it's a burden to be one of the few. Why do we need to be the role models all the time? It's not our fault we are one of the few; that's an institutional, organizational, and societal problem. It's not our weight to carry. Because there are not many who look like us, everything we do is more visible: both good and bad. We are keenly aware of the perceptions and potential biases against us, so we do our best to quell, anticipate, and respond to them proactively.

The stakes are higher for us. Shonda Rhimes, the powerhouse creator and writer behind *Grey's Anatomy*, *Bridgerton*, *How to Get Away with Murder*, and *Scandal* knew those stakes well. There is a scene in *Scandal*, when Olivia Pope (played by Kerry Washington) tries to explain to her boyfriend, Jake, why she can't just run off, marry him, and leave her career behind. She shouts: "Mediocrity is not an option for me!" For Olivia, leaving behind a career she worked tirelessly to build was a nonstarter. The underlying message was that as a White man, Jake couldn't understand the significance of that. To leave behind what she had built and all it meant would feel like a mediocre life to her. Like Olivia, we're building legacies—through not only our children but also our careers. And legacies aren't built on mediocrity, accepting the status quo, or settling. Many of us are the first in our families to do what we're doing, and we're creating a new reality for the generations coming after us. Because of that sense of purpose, it often feels like there is no other option for us but to continue to grin and bear it, as one of the few.

THE IDENTITY TAX

If the triple whammy from our cultural expectations wasn't enough, extensive research shows women and women of color are frequently subjected to stereotypes and biases in the workplace. Those stereotypes and biases lead us to feel like we need to work even harder. We feel pressure to prove ourselves over and over, to achieve endlessly, to be perfect, to be taken seriously, and to advance in our careers.

Consider the double standard. Women of color face higher standards for their behavior and performance than their White or male peers. This creates a situation where we're less likely to speak up for fear of being judged harshly or criticized.[2] We also have to grapple with the "identity tax," which is the extra effort and energy that women of color and others from underrepresented groups have to expend to overcome biases and stereotypes in the workplace.[3]

Again, the research on this is extensive.

- A study in the *Harvard Business Review* found that women of color are more likely than White women to feel the need to be seen as competent, and they are often held to higher standards than their White colleagues. They are presumed to be less qualified despite their credentials, work product, or business results.[4]

- Women of color, especially Black women and Latinas, experience "prove-it-again" bias at significantly higher levels than their White counterparts. They have to repeatedly provide evidence of their competence to be seen as equally competent and to receive the same recognition and respect.[5]

- A study by Leanin.org found that compared to White women, Black women are more than three times as likely and Latinas and Asian women are twice as likely to hear people express surprise at their language skills or other abilities.[6]

- One study in the *Asian American Journal of Psychology* found that Asian-American women are subjected to stereotypes that they are quiet, passive, and lacking leadership qualities, which lead them to feel invisible and marginalized.[7]

- McKinsey & Lean In's Women in the Workplace 2023 Report found that many women of color choose not to speak up or share an opinion to avoid seeming difficult or aggressive to their colleagues.[8] Black women in particular face persistent negative stereotypes and biases and report being more heavily scrutinized, having their authority and credibility questioned.[9] In one study, 86 percent of Black women reported changing their style of dress to "fit in" to corporate cultural standards of appearance.[10]

These workplace realities manifest when we're frequently denied the same advancement opportunities as others. It's when the law firm partner turns to you in a meeting and essentially says you aren't qualified to write a direct examination outline for your client's key witness, when the only other available associates at the table are two White men with no more experience than you. Yes, that's happened to me.

Can you imagine the fire I felt in my belly to crush that outline and prove that partner wrong? And can you imagine how sweet it was, two days later, to hear the lead trial partner read my outline out loud to the whole trial team (including the partner who said I shouldn't be the one to draft it) and express how good it was?

I don't share this story to show I proved that partner wrong. I share it to highlight that our experiences in the workplace are not simply created by how we think about them. We're subjected to unfair treatment that is not experienced by White men.

In my example, the partner thought my two White male colleagues (who were at the same level in the firm as me) could do it better. He didn't explicitly state that, but that's what he meant. The only difference between me and them was I was not White, and I was not a man. And the truth was, I had proven, through my work history, that I was a better fit for the assignment—and then I showed them again when I nailed the outline. The partner's discrimination against me was not on me; it was on him. The only thing I could control and had power over was my response to it. But it was mentally and emotionally draining. It's hard when you feel like you often have to navigate these types of situations.

PREGNANCY DISCRIMINATION

In addition to the realities of stereotypes and biases, research shows that women of color are more likely than White women to experience harassment and discrimination in workplaces, including being paid much less and being passed over for promotions despite having equal or greater career ambition because of their identities.[11]

I can attest to this firsthand. When I was pregnant with my

second child, I applied for an adjunct faculty position for the first-year writing program at a prestigious law school in Boston. The final interview was with a male, White professor who oversaw the program. When we sat down, he praised my resume and acknowledged I had the requisite experience for the position. He also remarked how highly others at the school spoke of my work and of me. Then, very quickly, he voiced his "concern" that I might not be able to manage my full-time job and teach writing to first-year students once my second child was born. He said he wasn't sure it was the "right time" for me, even though the teaching position was set to begin after maternity leave, when my child would be four months old. The professor's concerns outweighed my qualifications, and I didn't get that faculty position.

Let's set aside the irony that a *law professor* discriminated against me because I was a pregnant mother. He should've known better than to say any of that. What really got me was that he condescendingly indicated I was incapable of managing my life. But it wasn't his place to have an opinion about it and it certainly wasn't his decision to manage; it was and will always be mine.

That law professor's assumptions about my ability to manage a teaching position, a full-time job, and two children are like when women return from caregiver leave and they're denied visible projects, opportunities, or promotions. Decision makers, typically men, often don't believe mothers can truly excel at the work at the same pace (or want to do the work) while managing their other responsibilities. They assume that because you're a mother now, you aren't going to be as committed to the work, which for high-achieving women sounds ridiculous. *Have they met us?* Come on. We'd like to do both. To be clear, our workplaces don't typically provide the support structures for mothers (and fathers) to work and parent the way that works best for them to ensure high performance at work and present parents at home. But fathers don't have to prove wrong the assumption that they aren't as committed to their work after they become parents; mothers do.

MICROAGGRESSIONS HAVE A MACRO IMPACT

The frequency with which women of color and moms of color are subjected to discrimination and microaggressions in the workplace, as I was, takes a toll over time. Microaggressions are comments, actions, or slights rooted in discrimination and bias that may often, yet not always, appear more subtle and unintentional but can have a negative impact on a person's well-being and career.[12] For instance, asking a woman of color, "Where are you really from?" or "Is that your real hair?" (the insult type of microaggression) or telling a woman of color, "I'm colorblind. I don't see skin color. We're all just people." (the invalidation type of microaggression) are examples of microaggressions many of us have experienced.[13] Being confused for another person of color is also common. Black and Asian women are seven times more likely than White women to be confused with someone of the same race and ethnicity.[14]

Motherhood aside, women of color in the workplace are much more likely than White women to face "othering" microaggressions that reinforce negative stereotypes or make them feel like outsiders.[15] For instance, Black women have reported experiencing microaggressions related to their hair or appearance and in addition to their perceived competence, judgment, and emotional state.[16] These microaggressions are linked to higher levels of depression, lower self-esteem, lower job satisfaction, and a decreased sense of belonging in the workplace.[17]

Asian-American women are subjected to microaggressions that often take the form of perceived exoticism or objectification, among others, and as a result, they report increased stress levels and negative impacts on their self-esteem and psychological well-being.[18] A study in the *Journal of Latinx Psychology* found that Latinas reported experiencing microaggressions related to their accents, skin tone, and cultural practices.[19] That study along with others found that such microaggressions were associated with high levels of stress and lower levels of well-being.[20]

Mispronouncing the names of women of color is a common microaggression. When a person mispronounces your name, it makes you feel like your identity is not respected or valued. A recent study showed that 25 percent of people of color felt discriminated against when their names were mispronounced, 21 percent of Hispanics felt unimportant, and 19 percent of Asians felt self-conscious when it happened.[21] It's particularly harmful for women of color because we already face bias and discrimination related to our race, ethnicity, gender, and status as mothers. It also creates the additional burden of constantly having to correct others and feel like we have to adapt to a dominant culture that doesn't value our identity. This is evidenced by the adoption of more mainstream names or English pronunciations of names to make it "easier" for White colleagues or friends. Studies have shown name mispronunciations contribute to anxiety, stress, and shame, and can impact feelings of belonging and inclusion at work.[22] When someone takes the time and effort to learn and correctly pronounce your name, they're communicating respect and value for your identity.

In true Dominican fashion, my name is a mixture of my parents' names and it's 1,000 percent made-up. My mother's first name is Providencia (Provi for short). My father's name is Arismendi (Aris for short). They took the "Ari" from Aris and the "vi" from Provi to make: "Arivi." My parents knew the *i* in Spanish sounds like the "ee" sound in English. To achieve the same sound in Spanish, they (with the help of my glorious aunt) changed the "vi" at the end of Arivi to "vee." As a result, my name became Arivee. The most common mispronunciations are Ari-vay, Arrive, and Avery.

Name mispronunciations are the story of my life. I cannot remember a time, from childhood through present day, when I didn't have to correct someone's pronunciation. My mother taught me to pronounce it in Spanish and always roll the *r*, and not to Americanize it by removing that critical piece. I've always done that, and you know what I've learned? People who care learn how to pronounce my name. They may not nail the rolled *r*, but they try. That's what matters to me. When someone makes an effort, it gives me an increased sense of belonging.

The bottom line is that microaggressions make women of color feel psychologically and often physically unsafe. And when women feel psychologically unsafe, it's more difficult to take risks, share new ideas, or raise concerns. Research shows that 78 percent of women adjust the way they look or act in an effort to protect themselves at work. The Women in the Workplace 2023 Report by McKinsey & Leanin.org found that: "The stress caused by these dynamics cuts deep. Women who experience microaggressions—and self-shield to deflect them—are three times more likely to think about quitting their jobs and four times more likely to almost always be burned out."[23]

THE LEADERSHIP VOID

In addition, women, and especially women of color, are significantly underrepresented in leadership roles in corporate America.[24] I know this isn't new to you. Despite not seeing anyone who looks like us in senior leadership positions, we have ambitious plans and the desire to advance.

Consider this:

- Compared with 27 percent of White women, 41 percent of women of color want to be top executives.

- In 2022, McKinsey found that women occupied only 26 percent of C-suite positions, and women of color even lower at 5 percent.

- For senior vice president and vice president positions, the numbers weren't much better at 6 percent for women of color in SVP positions, and 8 percent for women of color in VP positions.[25]

- Women leaders, and women of color in particular, lead more initiatives to support employee well-being and diversity, equity, and inclusion work that is shown to improve employee retention and satisfaction. Forty percent of women leaders say their DEI contributions are not recognized. Thus, they are spending more energy and time on work that is not as visible, acknowledged, or valued, on top of all the other commitments they are juggling.

- Women have become more overworked than men in leadership, 43 percent of women leaders are burned out, compared with only 31 percent of men at the same level.[26]

Women of color who don't necessarily aspire to senior leadership are nonetheless hungry for new challenges, and they long for something more, something that excites and energizes them. Many have reached a point in their careers where they want to try something different. They may be looking for a role that provides more intellectual or creative stimulation or a position that allows them to pursue a different set of interests.

They also may seek a career change because they want to align their work with their personal values or sense of purpose. They may be looking for a role that would be better for their peace of mind and isn't as anxiety inducing and stressful, often due to unrealistic expectations from top leaders or clients where everything is urgent, all of the time. Or they may be looking for a role that allows them to live a lifestyle that doesn't require such long hours, regardless of the financial benefits.

According to a 2022 Gallup study, four out of ten workers in the United States report their job has either a "somewhat negative" or "extremely negative" impact on their mental health.[27] And women are more likely than men to report poor or fair mental health including depression.[28]

We might think this is "just the way it is," as I was told at that woman of color lawyer conference, but again, that mindset gives too much power away. Each one of us has the ability to see the systemic and real barriers in front of us and respond in a way that works for us. We have the ability to shift our mindset, be intentional with our actions and choices, and we have more agency than we think.

Let's Be Honest . . .

- What experiences have you had with stereotypes, biases, and/or discrimination at work, or have you observed others have?
- How have those experiences impacted your performance? Do they push you to work even harder or retreat, or to cope in another way?
- Have you ever had experiences where you felt psychologically unsafe or like you didn't belong? How did/do you respond in those situations?

Self-Worth: It's an Inside Job

"So long as you're still worried about what others think of you, you are owned by them. Only when you require no approval from outside yourself can you own yourself."

—Oprah Winfrey

Given the cultural expectations, the expectations we place on ourselves, and the workplace realities that professional women of color face, it's no wonder our internal monologue might be a little whacky. We're getting it from every direction externally and there's still our own brains, driving or dunking us at every turn. Momhood, the ancestral (and living) voices around me, and my growing dissatisfaction with my big-time legal career created a perfect storm of internal chatter after my son was born.

LOOKING WITHIN

I started to dig into why I was feeling the way I did about being a new mother with a dominant professional identity. I slowly became aware that my definition of myself was heavily dependent on the level of my performance and productivity, what partners and colleagues at work thought of me and whether they approved of me and my work.

The Praise Paradox

For most of my life, I was "good" in the eyes of everyone else around me. I grinded, like I was taught, and the grind paid off. I was rewarded with good grades, going to a top college and law school, passing the bar, practicing at large law firms, and obtaining prestigious clerkships and positions in the corporate world. I worked hard for those opportunities, and aside from being rewarded with achievements, I was also rewarded with praise from my mentors, community, family, network, and colleagues.

There was nothing wrong with receiving praise from the people who cared about me, worked with me, and invested their time and energy into my development. Being celebrated for my accomplishments felt good, albeit often awkward because I had not made a practice out of recognizing and celebrating my big or small wins. But it also always felt a little egotistical or icky, and never really felt like a "big deal." There was always so much more I wanted to do, and I was focused on the next thing I wanted to reach for.

Though I continued striving to achieve more and more, somewhere along the way, I started to tether that external praise, performance, and productivity with my self-worth. I felt this need to constantly demonstrate my worth through tangible, objective achievements. Mostly, I sought validation from others, like colleagues, to feel my efforts were recognized and valued.

Relying on external validation and the insatiable need to constantly achieve and produce was a recipe for suffering, because it allowed others to dictate how I felt. I gave too much power away by attaching how I felt about myself to performing at work and what people said about my work.

The issue was not that people praised me; rather, the issue is what I let that praise mean to

> Relying on external validation and the insatiable need to constantly achieve and produce was a recipe for suffering.

me and what I attached to it (my self-worth). It made me feel validated, good enough, and smart enough. While productivity and putting in the work to succeed can be a strength, it became my Achilles' heel when it came at my personal expense. That's because when you stop performing and achieving, the source for your worth dries up.

My experience, though it felt singular at the time, was not unique. Women of color often focus on overperforming to prove we're worthy, that we deserve our place among our peers. We spend too much energy on what others think of us and whether people like us and our work. We make our work a measure of our value.

But we can't beat ourselves up about this. No one taught us how to wrestle with feelings of self-doubt because of the spaces we enter. No one taught us how to navigate an environment where very few next to us and above us look like us or can relate to our background or life experience. For many of us, we were trailblazers by default. If we were lucky, we had a few mentors early on in our careers and we learned through trial and error, but we have the bumps, bruises, and scars to prove it.

When I internalized production and performance as the source of my self-worth and value, I crossed the line and made myself vulnerable to exactly what I ultimately experienced as a new mother. When I no longer had that external praise and positive reinforcement, my source for validation went away, and I was unmoored. I'd given up too much control.

That Gnawing Mom Guilt

The truth? The first six months of being a mother forced me to face myself. It was just me and the baby most days. I was only mothering. I was not lawyering, which is what I had done my entire career until then. Lawyering was who I was, but I allowed it to define all of who I was, instead of only a part of me.

So, when becoming a mother challenged that definition, it bothered me. Then it angered me. I got resentful, and I was sleep deprived. I felt like my world was closing in on me, at a time society and well-meaning friends and family say should be the most beautiful and happiest time in our lives. I felt guilty that my experience as a new mother didn't match how people expected me to feel. When I went back to work, the guilt morphed from feeling bad about not enjoying new motherhood to the expected degree to feeling like I wasn't home enough to give my child the attention and care he needed.

Despite extensive research on mom guilt, the Merriam-Webster dictionary has not yet caught up with the times and crafted a definition. The Cleveland Clinic defines mom guilt as "the feelings of guilt and shame some people feel when they don't live up to their own or others' expectations in their role as a parent. It's like an internal dialogue that tells you you're failing as a caregiver."[1]

Mom guilt arises in a wide range of situations, like when you feel like you're not spending enough quality time with your children. You worry you might hurt your relationship with your child or their well-being if you're not able to attend important events or milestones like a recital, game, or even taking them to practice. Be it externally or internally generated, you feel like you're not living up to the expectation of what a "good mother" would do, and you personally want to be there with and for your child.

Many women I've talked to about this express dual guilt, what psychologists call work-family guilt.[2] Women may feel guilty when they aren't working, especially around the evening hours when they're having dinner with their kids and putting them to bed, and then they feel guilty when work takes over and they have to miss a child's event or pick up or drop off because of work. Maybe you feel guilty for leaving your children crying when you have to travel for work, or go for a solo weekend, or spend a weekend with your girlfriends, or with your partner.

Even now, years after the birth of my son, my six-year-old daughter often clings to my legs when I'm heading out the door to go work out. She tells me she wants to spend time with me, that she misses me, and that she doesn't want me to go. I remind her that I need to take care of myself so I can take care of her the way she deserves, and although I feel bad about leaving her crying at home, I need to move my body for me. And I leave the house.

The way we experience guilt could be more subtle. It could show up when you're thinking about work and all your emails and to-dos while you're with your kids or your favorite people. You feel shame that you're with them and should be enjoying them, but you can't stop thinking about that email you need to respond to, or the work you have to do. That shame is a manifestation of guilt. You can also feel resentment toward your own loved ones, when you're responding on your phone to an email, but your partner or child wants your attention at the same time. You want them to leave you alone so you can just finish what you're doing, and then you feel guilt and shame for wanting that and reacting the way you do, as you're often frustrated in those moments.

Nonetheless, how we manage mom guilt can have a significant impact on our mental health and well-being, and it can lead to increased stress, anxiety, and burnout.[3] Women of color experience mom guilt in unique and often intersectional ways shaped by race, ethnicity, and cultural backgrounds. For instance, one study showed that because of cultural and gender expectations for Black women to spend more time on caregiving, family, and household management, than their careers, work-family conflict intensified as compared to that experienced by men.[4] Other research shows that cultural and gender expectations imposed on Latina mothers contribute to feelings of maternal guilt and stress.[5] Specifically, they deify previous generations of self-sacrificing mothers in their families as superior mothers against whom Latina mothers in the study render themselves failures.[6] Latina mothers in the study also strived to manage conflicting cultural norms to be a self-sacrificing mother who also is educated, has a career, and is financially secure.[7]

Though it's comforting, to a degree, to know that many working mothers suffer from mom guilt or some form of it, that knowledge doesn't provide much guidance as far as how to navigate it.

Just Be Grateful

Most of the time, we're told, "Just be grateful" for all you have. The "just be grateful" clapback you tell yourself (or someone tells you) is different from the practice of gratitude that is a powerful tool for mental health and well-being. Renowned shame and vulnerability researcher Brené Brown defines gratitude as an emotion and a *practice* that "reflects our deep appreciation for what we value, what brings meaning to our lives, and what makes us feel connected to ourselves and others."[8] Studies have found that practicing gratitude (i.e., daily gratitude meditations, journaling, art) increases positive emotions and self-esteem, enhances life satisfaction and well-being, and improves relationships with others.[9] Expressing gratitude allows you to focus on the good in your life, cultivate positive emotions, foster deeper connections with others, and feel better about yourself. This is great news, right?

But here's something you should know: gratitude isn't the solve-everything answer.

It appears like a win-win, and it certainly can be, until you start using gratitude as a weapon of shame against yourself to keep you from acting on your true desires and needs. "Just be grateful" is what we tell ourselves when we desire more. We think of what we want or need, and then pull back. We silence that part of ourselves. We shut it down and convince ourselves that what we have is good enough, and then we feel guilty for wanting more. We may also feel afraid of losing what we already have.

Compounding the fear and guilt is the cultural reality that our ancestors and parents had it harder. If you were told you were "too sensitive," "exaggerating," or "dramatic" when you expressed your feelings as a child, it was probably the result of parents who did, in fact, have it harder in certain aspects, and who had no tools to deal with any of it. They were probably told those exact words or received those messages as children.

For many first-generation and women of color professionals, we often think of the opportunities and privileges we have that others in our family and communities didn't have. That awareness can quickly turn into holding ourselves back from feeling the joy, alignment, and fulfillment in work and life without the constant internal struggle. The exemplar matriarch inspires and motivates us, but also presents an unrealistic model for how we experience work and family today.

We tell ourselves to "just be grateful" because we "already have so much, more than they had." This may be true, but gratitude should not be used as an excuse, a mechanism, or a default mindset to play it small, to be okay with less, to be quiet, and to accept things because that's "just the way it is." Hell no.

> Gratitude should not be used as an excuse, a mechanism, or a default mindset to play it small.

GETTING CURIOUS

When I was on maternity leave with my son, and after I lost it from exhaustion and inner conflict, I began spending every free moment of my time researching, reading, writing, and reflecting on my life. I wanted to understand why I felt like something was missing. I was longing for more, so I took time to get clear on who I was and who I wasn't. I got clearer and clearer on what *I wanted*, rather than what was expected of me.

When I noticed I was frustrated, angry, and resentful, I got curious about why. Why did all of this bother me so much? What was happening to me? What was changing in me? Who the hell was I? What did I really want out of my life? I thought I was having some kind of midlife crisis, but I was only thirty-two. So, not midlife, but new-mama-life crisis for sure.

I started writing down my thoughts and feelings in a journal. The theme in the beginning was always the same: *I'm exhausted, and I want to go back to work. I miss talking to adults all day. I love my son, and I need to get out of here.* Whether you're first-generation (like me) or not, you know these can be the toughest conversations you have with yourself.

Around this time, I started researching (translation: Googled) topics related to being a new mom, being a lawyer and a mom, having an identity crisis after a baby, and so many other iterations. I also came across two books that changed my life: *The Gifts of Imperfection* by Brené Brown and *A Return to Love* by Marianne Williamson.

The Gifts of Imperfection gutted me. It highlighted the thoughts that make us feel inadequate and the root of those thoughts: expectations others have of us that we've internalized. Brené shares many ways to step into who you really are, including how to practice compassion with ourselves and embrace who we are underneath all the external BS. It takes courage and being willing to connect deeply with yourself and others.

A Return to Love was all about how you're enough, because you're a human who exists. Nothing is needed to make you worthy; you're inherently worthy and enough. Marianne Williamson's main point is that we were all created in love, and we need to love ourselves, treat ourselves with kindness and compassion, and understand how powerful we are in this moment to make decisions that can change the course of our lives.

I was raised Catholic and attended a Jesuit Catholic university, but along the way, I lost why my faith mattered to me. When Marianne Williamson speaks about being created in love, she's talking about God—God created you, so you have inherent worth. The fact that you were created makes you worthy. It makes you an original. It makes you unique. You don't have to do anything extra to earn your worthiness, originality, or uniqueness.

From there, I went on a full-on, nerd-out personal development book rampage. I read everything I could get my hands on: Brené Brown's *Daring Greatly*; Jack Canfield's *The Success Principles*; Wayne Dyer; Steven Covey; Jen Sincero's *You are a Badass*; Don Miguel Ruiz's classic, *The Four Agreements*; and more. I also started to reengage with my spirituality and the belief that the greater world was sending messages to step into what the universe was calling me to do and who it was calling me to be.

I know this may sound weird to some people, but I started talking to God like I was praying, but not at bedtime. I talked to him at random moments, especially when I was frustrated. And to this day, I do that. I don't attend church often, but my relationship with God is one of the reasons I believe in human potential and goodness so deeply. And trust me, me and God have been through some shit. But after I had my son, I felt I was missing the lightness and energy of being connected to something greater out there: God, or the universe, and something deeper within myself.

Now, there's something you should know about me. I believe in doing books, not only reading them. This means I write notes in my books, tab them, and I write about what I've learned in a journal or in the book itself (told you I nerded out). I applied certain principles to my life, and I let go of other beliefs that were holding me back.

Here are a few of the life lessons I learned to apply to my daily reality to gain clarity, get more anchored to find more fulfillment, alignment, and joy.

- **Be honest with yourself about how you feel and what you think.** Ask yourself what makes you have certain feelings and thoughts? Where do they come from? What events, people, or activities trigger them more than others, and why? Sit with your feelings and face them, instead of stuffing them down or ignoring them. You can't out-work and distract yourself from your feelings forever.

- **Get real about your values and priorities given where you are today,** not where you used to be or wish you were.

- **Anchor into what gives you a sense of meaning and purpose in life.** If you don't know, that's okay. Start exploring.

- **Be clear about what you want, your goals, and your vision for your life.** Saying you want to feel peace doesn't cut it.

You need a vision of what having peace looks like. It will look different from others' visions. That's the point.

- **Release the weight of societal, familial, and cultural expectations** you internalized as a child and brought with you into adulthood.

- **Release the unrealistic expectations you've imposed on yourself.** Let go of the feeling that you have to do it all, for everyone, every day. You can't and shouldn't do everything. It's not sustainable in the long term.

- **Notice how you talk to yourself.** Beating yourself up doesn't come from a place of love; it comes from the fear that you're inadequate. You're inherently whole and worthy of everything you are and everything you desire.

- **Quit the comparison game.** You have no idea what someone else is going through. Don't compare the images of other people's lives with your real one.

- **Unlearn the people-pleasing behavior** you learned as a child, especially if you're a woman of color and child of immigrant parents. I get it. You just wanted to stay out of the way and do what you were told to limit stress in the home and be less of a burden.

- **Believe in the changes you desire.** Any change in habits and daily actions first requires a fierce belief in why you're doing it and a mindset shift, from one of impossibility to one of possibility.

- **Pay attention to how you feel in your body and spirit** when you're making decisions, going to work, interacting with people, and experiencing things. Your body holds wisdom that needs to be heard and listened to.

- **Choose to be your best advocate.** Ask for what you need and want. Do not have the general expectation that others can read your mind and guess what you need and want.

- **Harness your self-agency.** As a woman of color and a mother, you face systemic challenges. At the same time, you have the power, adaptability, and perseverance to navigate these challenges and make things happen for yourself.

- **You don't have to have it all figured out.** Do the best you can with integrity and stay true to who you are and what you most need and want.

- **You deserve to live a life you love.** There will be difficult moments and challenges, because life be life-ing sometimes. But you deserve to free yourself from the burdens and suffering that cause you to be at war with yourself. Suffering does not have to be your steady, normal state. Neither does incessant worry, confusion, or stagnation. As hard as it is to believe, your steady, normal state can be filled with more joy, fulfillment, and inner alignment.

In all the books I read, one message was always the same.

Any change starts with self-awareness. Self-awareness leads to learning, which leads to enhanced clarity, shifting of beliefs and thoughts, managing your emotions, and ultimately, action and results. If it seems simple, it is. But it's not easy. Because life is complex and so

> Any change starts with self-awareness.

are humans. Our human experience isn't linear; it's a journey of peaks and valleys, twists and turns. Point A to Point B is rarely a straight incline without dips or spikes.

CALLING BULLSHIT

A big part of my personal development deep dive was listening to podcasts like *The Marie Forleo Podcast* (about building a life and business you love); the *Good Life Project* (about what it can mean to live a good life) by Jonathan Fields, former New York City "big law" lawyer turned yoga business owner and podcast entrepreneur and his wife, Stephanie Fields; and *The Life Coach School* by master life coach, Brooke Castillo.

Those three podcasts and books I read led to me participating in coaching programs as a client, where I worked on being brutally honest with myself about my needs, wants, values, and priorities. This work required being open and willing to make the changes that would generate more self-acceptance and self-love. And with the newfound clarity, I slowly began to have more alignment and joy in my personal and professional life. (A year later, I enrolled in a coaching certification program focused on High-Performance™ in life—i.e., sustaining personal alignment, joy, growth, and abundance in all parts of your life over the long term.)

The self-analysis learned through the coaching program was enough to guide me through the transition back to work and slightly beyond. When my son was almost a year old and finally sleeping through the night, I landed in a place where I made the mental space to seriously consider what was next for me. I enjoyed the people I worked with at the law firm. I loved researching, writing, and practicing the skills that are exercised over and over as a litigation attorney.

There was just one problem: I didn't like the substance of what I was doing. The subject matter (securities litigation) didn't excite me at all. I did it because, at law firms, the billable hour is king. If you aren't billing, you're underutilized, and that's a no-no. At law firms, you have to "make your hours."

When I dug deep into why I was still at the firm, I realized there were three main reasons.

1. It paid well and afforded me a lifestyle I had become accustomed to. (I had not seen that much money in my life!)

2. I was playing it safe. I knew the law firm game and could play it, and I didn't want to learn to play another game in a different work environment. I didn't want to start over and have to rebuild my reputation somewhere new.

3. I really liked the people I worked with.

I worked hard because I cared deeply about excelling at my craft and about my clients, who as a senior associate, were often the partners with whom I worked. My peers were down-to-earth, smart, fun people. There was no stuffiness in our office, and I appreciated that. You hear horror stories of stuck-up law firm lawyers, and although they surely exist, I was fortunate to not work with any of them.

So, I applied to be a federal prosecutor thinking it would be challenging and rewarding personally. I'll spare you the entire story, but I ultimately withdrew my application on the day of my final interview with the US attorney (after the most challenging interview process ever). Around this time, I'd been having conversations with my partner mentor and the head litigation partner in my office. They told me I could be "up for partner" the following year. I thought it was too early and told them as much. They said, no—it's the right time, if it's what you want. I said I'd think it over, but I didn't need to.

The feeling I got was straight up dread. It was definitely not excitement. Why do they tell you more than a year in advance? So they can help prepare you, and so you have the opportunity to do everything you can to give yourself the best chance of making partner. This includes working with the right partners, working on the right matters, and making sure you've proven all you need to prove.

I didn't want to do that. Not because I knew it would be a challenge (I've never shied away from hard work), but because I simply didn't want partnership anymore. I wanted it earlier in my career, especially when it looked kind of glamorous. The women partners I knew were straight up badassess, and I loved that. But I didn't want that life or that lifestyle. I didn't want to have to make it rain with new clients. I didn't want to have to be available 24/7. I didn't want to have to respond to clients or fellow partners at all hours. I knew that level of accessibility would mess with me mentally, and I wouldn't be able to feel the freedom to rest when I needed rest, to be fully present with family and friends, and to take real vacations. It would've created too much of a distraction anytime I wasn't working. I know myself well enough to know I need space from work at times and don't want to be beholden to a laptop constantly. No amount of money would make that worth it for me.

The only reason I would have gone for partnership was because I'd worked very hard for it up to that point, and because there were very few Latina partners at my firm, and Boston had close to zero Latina law firm partners. I felt a responsibility to show my community it could be done. But I was tired of being the one all the damn time. And I was tired of being the one who had to trail blaze. The expectation that I would do it bothered me. It wasn't all in my head.

There were men and women I looked to for advice at the time, and only one of them told me that *I had to want it* to go for it. The others said: "Make partner and then you can go do anything you want." I was tired of hearing this too. *Wait until you check this or that box to then go live your life and do what you "really" want.* I was calling bullshit on it. And I heard the typical: *But you're making so much money. You have the financial stability and security others would do anything to have.* I was calling bullshit on that too. The fact that others would do anything for the opportunity in front of me had nothing to do with what *I wanted.* They weren't living my life; I was.

I began to anchor into the belief that I had the power to make decisions for myself, decisions that served me and were aligned with who I was becoming. I also started releasing so many expectations I felt burdened by. They were only making things harder for me.

Let's Be Honest . . .

- What is one part of your life you've been avoiding or distracting yourself from? What makes that part so uncomfortable for you?

- What decisions have you made that, looking back, you see didn't reflect what you really wanted at the time?

- What's one decision you can make right now that you've been delaying out of fear of not knowing how it'll turn out, or fear of not doing what you "should" or "could" do, fear of what others might think, including those closest to you, or the previous version of yourself?

The 4-Part Framework

*"So many of us invest a fortune making ourselves
look good to the world, yet inside we are falling apart.
It's time to invest on the inside."*

—Iyanla Vanzant

Nothing about working in a law firm was different, but I was different. I had changed on the inside. I was not the same person I was before my son was born or when I started my legal career. So, I left. I said goodbye to my old dreams because they weren't mine anymore. I said goodbye to the cultural and societal expectations that weren't mine to carry anymore. I said goodbye to avoiding the truth and to playing small.

BECOMING A COACH

I'm here to tell you there is so much joy, fulfillment, and alignment waiting for you because I'm an example of it. When I gained clarity that being a lawyer at a law firm was not enough for me, I left and joined a biotech company's legal and compliance group.

Around that time, I had been working with a Life and High-Performance™ coach.

Coaching gave me the space to explore parts of myself I'd avoided confronting my entire life, such as feelings of unworthiness, seeking validation through my work, and struggling with self-love or being kind to myself when I fell short of my own expectations. As I've shared, I learned many harmful thinking patterns and beliefs that my coach and I worked to unravel, unpack, and reset. This work increased my self-awareness and taught me how to

- Be honest and listen to myself over the voices all around me.
- Call bullshit on the weight of expectations that were crushing my spirit.
- Release myself from trying to be everything to everyone all the time and give myself permission to choose myself.
- Develop and invest in myself for myself instead of for others.
- Lead myself away from an unfulfilling role into a position better suited to my interests and passions.

I felt myself changing in small ways, and big ways too. The negative, self-loathing thoughts stopped spiraling. I placed less weight on others' opinions of me. Over time, I stopped seeking (and relying on) external validation to feel good about myself.

Coaching changed my life, and I became deeply interested in giving the gift of self-discovery, awareness, and change to other women. But I didn't want to help just anyone; I wanted to specifically focus on other women like me: women lawyers, first-generation and women of color professionals, and mothers who are ambitious and driven in their careers. I recognized that personal development and self-help space does not represent our unique challenges and circumstances. While working in-house, I became a certified Life and High-Performance Coach™, with both research-based and validated coaching certification programs.

Three years later, I wanted to align my professional life with my personal one, and knew I was not exercising my strengths and using my gifts the way I longed to do. I decided to leave the legal and compliance group and move to a leadership role in human resources. This was not a random decision. Human resources allowed me a professional avenue to help our talent grow and develop so they can be their best and flourish. It's much like what I do for my coaching clients outside of work but with a different lens.

Through my independent coaching work with high-performing women and professional women of color, I noticed a few crucial themes, perspectives, and experiences continued to surface. (My legal training served me well in this regard, because I was essentially issue-spotting, which is when you read or hear a fact pattern and identify the legal issues, separating the facts that require your attention from the noise.) These women felt so similarly to the way I felt after my son was born; there was an automatic kinship.

Like me, they struggled to

- Recognize the season or stage of life they were in (i.e., new mother, mother of older children, mid-career, newly minted senior executive) and adjust accordingly.

- Be honest with themselves about the areas of their lives they were most satisfied and dissatisfied with and decide whether or not to do something about it.

- Explore and anchor themselves in their priorities, values, strengths, and sense of purpose and meaning, and set boundaries, for the love of all things!

- Set goals related to how they *wanted to feel* (less stress, stuck, or confused and more joy, calm, peace, fulfillment, and freedom) versus objective guideposts of success. They sometimes had both, but I found it always came back to a feeling.

- Allow others, including friends and family, to support them (i.e., they learned to ask for help), even though this behavior was not modeled for them growing up.

- Release the expectations of previous versions of themselves, and release the expectations of others, especially those of their culture, family, and the perceived "they."

- Bet on themselves, which is risky and scary and goes against most messages they picked up and internalized as children about stability and security.

- Curb negative self-talk including self-judgment and fear of judgment and rejection from others.

- Stop feeling guilty for working when they weren't with their kids or for being with their kids when they "should" be working.

You'll notice the very first bullet point in this list refers to being in a particular "season of life." I learned this term when I was being coached, and it became an important touch point in my own coaching practice.

THE SEASONS OF LIFE

A season of life is a phase of your life journey characterized by specific circumstances, experiences, or challenges, and it holds opportunities for growth and development.[1] Each season of life can be defined by a variety of factors such as age range, career stage, raising children, caregiving for a parent, health, and personal growth, all of which impact our ability to achieve well-being and feel fulfillment.

For instance, your twenties might generally be about exploring who you are and beginning your career. Your thirties may be a season of navigating career aspirations and acceleration and possibly motherhood. By your late thirties, your body is starting to age. Your forties may be a season of navigating career changes and parenting, while focusing even more on what truly lights you up and gives you meaning. Your fifties may be a massive transition period when your children are close to graduating from high school or are going off to college. Many women may retire in their fifties and pursue "encore" careers. This is also the time when it might become necessary to begin caring for aging parents, which brings an entirely new set of emotions and challenges.

At the time of this writing, my three children are nine, six, and three. Each child and career pivot brought me into a new season of life, and I had to navigate each transition in a way that served me. Each time I transitioned from one season of life to the next, I had to learn to let go of the old me to step into the new me, and I had to honor what the new me

> I had to learn to let go of the old me to step into the new me.

needed and wanted. There was a constant push and pull and tension between seasons—that critical transition period where you aren't sure who the fuck you are, what is going on, or what just happened. Sometimes, we can't have what we want in the moment, and we have to be laser focused on our priorities in that particular season of life.

There is no blueprint for navigating these seasons as a mother who is also a woman of color in the workplace because we all have different desires, needs, resources, values, and perspectives. But just because there is no general blueprint doesn't mean we can't learn how to create and implement personal, customizable tools to navigate the inflection points with more self-agency and empowerment.

The thirties and forties—the season of life for moms who are concurrently pursuing their career ambitions—is all about managing multiple roles and responsibilities. I'm not going to sugarcoat it: this can feel like a real slog, sometimes. You're managing your career, raising your children, maintaining a household, nurturing your relationship with a partner (if you have one), and more.

Raising kids is straight up hard work. You work all day, and then you go home to work more by taking care of your kids. Especially with young children, you're often over-touched, over-called upon (Mommy, Mommy, Mommy), and over-needed (at least that's how it can feel). And please know, two things can very much be true at the same time, such as "maybe it would be nice if everyone left me alone for fifteen minutes" AND "I feel so freakin' lucky to have these kids, I could scream." Those types of conflicting thoughts are a thing. You would do anything for your children, but sometimes, things get hectic and you need a break. See, you're not alone! Trust me, I'm in the thick of it right now, too.

Each year brings about a new set of challenges and lessons to learn. You need to have more patience, there's more listening to do, and your kids seem to need more focused attention. If you have kids who are neurodivergent or have unique needs, this adds another layer of care and attention. They're changing and growing, and sometimes it feels like you're just trying to keep up. You don't have control over their growth or the humans they will become. You don't have control over how they'll be treated by others. But you're doing your damn best to ensure you've prepared your kids to go off into the world as responsible, independent, kind, compassionate, loving humans.

When it comes to your career during this season, you may have hit a plateau. Maybe you're experiencing a sense of stagnation and a lack of fulfillment, asking yourself: *How did I get here and do I really still want to do this?* Or do I really want partnership or to be a senior executive, even if it's available to me? Maybe your job lacks growth opportunities or new challenges. Maybe you feel good about where you are, and you're not looking to advance further up the ranks right now. Maybe you're thinking of a promotion, or a change in role, industry, or career. Maybe you've reentered the workforce from maternity leave or other caregiver leave. Maybe you're flirting with being an entrepreneur, if you aren't one already. Or maybe, just maybe, you're simply thinking about how you'll survive this week, or this day, with all that's on your plate at work and at home.

Because you've picked up this book, I know you're ambitious just like me. Overachieving is part of my DNA. Some of it is straight up survival/coping skills—which can be an asset in some cases (achieving stuff) and a liability in others (maintaining well-being and quality of life)—and some of it is just how I operate. But my overachieving nature is not exclusive to work or career-related behaviors. I bring my overachieving self to *everything*: my relationships, my kid time, planning, working out, and more. My high standards of excellence do not chill. So, if you strive to give your all at work *and* at home, I'm with you, sister . . . it's a lot.

You're not alone in feeling overwhelmed, trying to manage everything—and systemic barriers add to that overwhelm. As women of color, we experience work-family conflict differently than White women. Studies have shown, time and time again, work-family conflict is more intense and pervasive for women of color. This conflict is associated with lower levels of job and career satisfaction, higher levels of job stress, and greater levels of psychological distress.[2] One study showed work-family conflict was associated with high levels of depression and anxiety among women of color.[3] Thus, this season of life can rock us to the core.

Overcoming the struggle requires taking stock of where you are: both your season of life and your level of satisfaction in fixed areas of your life during this season. Our seasons of life transition from one to the next, even when we aren't fully ready for what may lie ahead. But when you're able to recognize these transitions and the season of life you're in, you're better able to accept it and stop resisting it. Once you accept what is, you can make decisions to better navigate your current season.

Resisting is more than wanting things to be different. Consider your life before kids. You might (not so secretly) long for your life the way it was, when things felt simpler. I often ask myself, *What was I doing before I had my first child?* I didn't realize how much free time I had! But I do know what I was doing: sleeping in on weekends, traveling, spending time with my favorite people, and working a lot. I did what I wanted, when I wanted. I didn't have to get home and stay there by an 8 p.m. curfew. I could grab an impromptu dinner with colleagues, friends, or my husband on a weekday.

While we're grateful for our children and our careers, we can still lament all the responsibilities at home and at work. There is no shame in that. Adulting, parenting, and navigating the ups and downs and twists and turns of life is no walk in the park. You're a human being who can long for something you had before, and who might sometimes be just done with all the responsibilities. I'd argue this is a common sentiment we don't talk enough about.

If you have a partner, partners can be a strong source of support. Too often, women share with me that their male partners aren't carrying their fair share of childcare and household management duties. If you and your partner both have high-powered careers—that didn't change simply because you had children. In your partnership, are you with someone who works from the early morning to late at night and knows you'll take care of things at home? Someone who doesn't do bedtime or who half-heartedly participates because they "have so much work to do"? Or, is your partner someone who can't be alone with the kids because "they are too much" or can't even change a poopy diaper? Is your partner unwilling (because it's about willingness, not ability) to take time off from work to get the kids to their doctor's appointments when they are sick or need to be picked up immediately from school? To those partners, I say with love, they need to grow up. And to you, I'd say start with a conversation with your partner. If conversations on your own don't lead to change, I'm a huge fan of couples therapy to work through things.

You and your partner made a mutual decision to be parents together. Parents are not part-time babysitters. They don't need to "help" more; they need to split parenting responsibilities. They are perfectly capable of learning how to take care of their own kids, just like they learned how to do everything else. They have to step up big-time. And to you I say, with love, you have to let go of the need to control everything and allow them the chance to step up.

Or, maybe you're someone who still does all the things you did before you had children: working long hours, volunteering, sitting on boards, and going out for on-the-whim dinners with colleagues and friends. You may be the person who says: "I'm not giving up anything just because I have kids." Operating this way is like trying to fit a square peg in a round hole because *things have changed.*

The women I work with want to do all the things because they love it. They genuinely want to do it all. But we can't do it all. We're humans with mental, emotional, and physical thresholds and competing obligations. None of us can "do it all"—the kids, the work, taking care of the home, the volunteering, etc. We aren't machines.

> Our phones need to be recharged to work, and so do we.

Our phones need to be recharged to work, and so do we. Wanting more simplicity, and then getting back to business, is different from operating as if you're still in your previous season.

I'm not saying you need to stop doing the things that light you up. I'm saying you need to focus on your non-negotiable priorities and pay far less attention to everything else. Every single season requires a fresh understanding of what parts of your life can align with those priorities, and what parts cannot. The sooner you can consciously identify the conflicting parts of your life and decide what level of tension you're okay with, the sooner you'll be able to accept (and embrace) your current season.

COMMIT TO CHANGE; COMMIT TO YOU

I want to be completely transparent about something. All the women I coach are ready to commit to a new way of living life, one step at a time. They want change yesterday and that desire can be seen in how they're showing up for themselves and their families. But they understand they have to do the work to create that change. The work doesn't involve massive steps at a time; in fact, our brains don't like big change. Our brains love what is familiar. When you challenge it to think differently, it interprets the challenge as a threat to your survival.

Do you believe a different way to live and work is possible? If you aren't open to the possibility, your brain will shut this book down. It will feed you all the reasons why change is impossible. Our brains are ridiculously good at giving us excuses. My love, before your brain shuts shit down and robs you of the opportunity to change your life, hear me out.

Change takes time, attention, awareness, and intentional work. It requires you to focus on how you think of the change, how much you want the change, and all the steps you'll take (very tiny, one at a time) to get there with patience and self-compassion. You have to be willing to engage with parts of you that haven't been uncovered yet: the thoughts and feelings you avoid or hide from. You have to be willing to experience the discomfort that comes with changing your life. You have to be open to the process.

As I see it, you have three options:

1. First, you can resist how you feel and what is happening in your life, which leads to a never-ending loop of dissatisfaction and stress. This is the least ideal option because you'll stay stuck where you are.

2. Second, you can choose to accept and make peace with what's going on for you and simply deal with it the best you can each day. There is no shame in this option. You take it one day at a time.

3. Or third, you can decide right here, right now, that life doesn't have to be this hard, or that you don't have to feel how you feel—whether it's stressed, stuck, confused, overwhelmed, lacking fulfillment, out of alignment—and you're open to believing it's possible to create the life and career that you feel so dang good in your soul.

I hope you're with me and choose option three. I know what I'm asking of you, and I recognize I wouldn't be able to help you, or any of the women I coach, if I had not gone through my own life seasons—if I hadn't made a commitment to change, and if I hadn't chosen option three. My coaching certifications, training, and coaching practice gave me a specific set of skills, which I'll share with you in the pages ahead, but that's not where the richest juice is. The richest juice is anchoring yourself in who you really are and coming to terms with what's true and not true about your current season.

A typical coaching conversation goes something like this

- Where are you now?
- Where do you want to go?
- What is in the way of getting there?

This is a bridging-the-gap type of coaching. While these three questions provide a baseline framework, my own transformations have taught me we need deeper work to even be able to answer those questions. We rarely talk about the unlearning we need to do to establish a new pattern of thinking and make it stick. (I've devoted all of Chapter 10 to the critical practice of unlearning.)

Recall, when I had my son, I was exhausted because he wasn't sleeping. Not being at work—where I received praise and validation—was killing me. I felt like I was dying inside. It may sound extreme, but that's the best way I can describe it. I thought: *Wait, so now I pop out a baby, and I'm just a mother? F' that.* When I was about to return to work, a family member suggested I step back from my career and stay home with the baby for a year. This time, I thought: *F' off. That's what you'd do, but not me.* But you know how it is. I didn't actually say that. Instead, I said, "Oh, thanks for the advice but that's not for me."

The truth is, I was desperate to find a way to align who I was on the inside with how my life looked on the outside. I was eager to tap into a deeper sense of purpose and fulfillment.

Maybe that's you. Maybe you're looking to align your values with your work and your everyday life. Maybe you're curious about how you can align who you are inside with your daily actions and habits. Maybe you're in the thick of motherhood and career acceleration, and you want to pump the breaks to check in and assess where you are, so you don't run yourself into the ground. Or maybe you're looking to step off the hamster wheel and get intentional about who you want to become and what you want to do next. Maybe you've reached a breaking point, where the weight of expectations, guilt, shame, and the responsibilities and obligations of work and family is getting to be too much to bear. Have you had a knees-to-floor moment where you hit an inflection point and weren't sure what to do, or where to go from there? You may find yourself in some combination of these scenarios. I certainly relate to all of them.

In the chapters ahead, I'm going to give you the tools to move from uncertainty and confusion into joy, fulfillment, and ease in your work and personal life. It's very hard to believe such a reality exists when you've been stuck at an inflection point or you're dealing with high levels of stress and running frantically from one task to the next. You might think: *How am I going to find the time for me, when I'm moving from one day to the next, to reach the end of the work week?* (And having the kids home all weekend is a whole other type of mental and emotional work.) But if I was able to move through it, and hundreds of women like you have, you can, too.

OUR ROAD MAP

You're still with me. Good! I'm glad you're here. I'm excited to share a 4-Part Framework that has helped me, and the women I work with, move from feeling stuck, uncertain, and confused to gaining clarity and finding joy and fulfillment in the current season of their lives. It is intended as a tool to use each time you reach a crossroads point in your life where you know something's gotta give, and you can't keep living the way you're living and working anymore. You want to figure out what's going on, what you truly need and want, and how to make all of that happen. By using the framework, you'll create alignment in how you show up each day for yourself, for those you love, and for your work.

I wish I could tell you that the framework came to me in a dream or that I had some alchemist-style vision, but that's not how it happened. It really came out of doing the work on myself. It's a blend of my own independent self-help research, my personal experience being coached, becoming certified in coaching, and my experience of working directly with hundreds of women. The combined collective struggle, knowledge, and unique gifts and insights that professional women of color have to give are mixed into this 4-Part Framework, which is easy to remember because each part begins with an *a*.

The 4 As are

1. **Assess**: Take stock of where you are. This is about assessing all the different areas of your life, assessing the season of life you're in, and deciding where to focus your attention and intention as you move forward. This requires being brutally honest with yourself.

2. **Activate**: Know your strengths, core values, and what gives you meaning and purpose. We are most powerful when we're exercising our strengths, operating in alignment with our core values, and feeling grounded in what gives us a sense of meaning and purpose. We're going to learn how to activate your strengths, core values, and your sense of meaning and purpose. This would include identifying the specific purpose your work or job serves.

3. **Ask**: What's your vision for your life in the future? We'll use a one-year time frame to start. Some say this is one of the most impactful parts of the framework because it brings your strengths, core values, and what gives you a sense of meaning and purpose to life through all your senses.

4. **Align**: This is where we put it all together. Align your strengths, core values, priorities, and sense of meaning and purpose with your daily actions to bring you closer to your vision.

You don't have to wait until you reach a breaking point to get started. Instead, you can be proactive. I'm here to show you how.

In Part 2: The 4-Part Framework in Action, I'm going to share practical ways to implement the 4 As as well as transformative stories of the women I've worked with, who did the work to gain clarity, alignment, and fulfillment. I'll share stories like Monica's, a mother who had her "dream job" but was unhappy and longed to fill her cup in a different way. You'll hear about women who ended up asking for and securing a promotion, who struggled with integrating life and work, but learned how to prioritize their well-being despite hectic schedules, and who were simply trying to figure out what they actually wanted and how to start going after it.

My hope is that these stories provide an extra dose of motivation and inspiration, and that they allow you to strengthen your belief that what you're longing for is possible.

My job is to challenge you with love and compassion. I know you deserve so much more than you may have given yourself the opportunity to realize. I also know you're likely way too hard on yourself. I'm here to help you break that cycle. I'm here to cheer you on. You got this, and I got you.

Before we jump in, let's agree on a few ground rules.

- Be open to learning a new perspective about things you think cannot be changed, i.e., "I'm a mom and corporate professional, so that means I'll never have time and I will always be tired."

- Be open to challenging beliefs that don't help you get closer to the life you want to live and the person you want to and can become. Ask yourself: *What's another perspective? What would it feel like to adopt that perspective? How would my approach change?*

- Pay attention to how you feel throughout this book, as I continue to invite you to take each step along the journey.

Resistance is a sign you need to get more curious and ask yourself: *What's underneath this tension I feel? What am I avoiding or suppressing? What am I afraid of?*

- Be open to exploring the truths you'll uncover in our work together. You know you best. Make this book work for you. You may want to read it cover to cover in one or two sittings and then come back to each section to do the work later. Or you may want to dig deeper and complete the exercises as you go. Do what works best for you. I'll encourage you to keep the momentum.

Before we dig in, I want to take a moment to acknowledge you for investing in yourself by picking up this book. By reading and interacting with it, you've become intentional about your decision to invest in your happiness, joy, and fulfillment. There is nothing else you need to get started. You're right where you need to be. You're here. You made it. Are you ready to change your life? I know I'm excited, too. Let's do it.

PART 2

THE 4-PART FRAMEWORK IN ACTION

ASSESS: Take Stock of Where You Are

"When you decide you truly do not ever want to feel a certain way again, you set out on a journey to self-awareness, learning and growth that has you radically reinvent who you are."

—Brianna Wiest

Some mornings, on the way to get my protein smoothie (I like getting fancy sometimes), I walk by a shiny, beautiful restaurant. From outside the floor-to-ceiling glass windows, you can see almost everything inside is white. Yes, white: white leather chairs, white linens on the tables, white walls, and a white hostess stand. And you can see the most delicate wine glasses, polished silverware, and napkins configured perfectly at each place setting. Each time I walk by, the first thing I think is, *Wow, my kids would tear this place up!*

The restaurant is way too white and fancy for kids. Clearly, the owners agree because of course, there's a small plaque on the door that says, "Fine Dining." When I hear "fine dining," I translate it to mean, "Parents, don't even think about bringing your kids in here." There's nothing wrong with this. Some dining experiences can only truly be enjoyed in the company of other adults. And for the most part, these days, that's not the kind of dining experience I'm having. Are you with me?

MY MCDONALD'S SEASON

I've Assessed where I am, and I'm in my McDonald's season. When you're a mother, choosing where to eat with your kids is a thing. You have to think long and hard about where you go. It's a conscious decision. A gazillion questions run through your mind as you consider the potential options. *What will my kids eat here? Does this restaurant have chicken nuggets or tenders? French fries? Chopped cucumbers or broccoli? Does it have apple juice? Is there pasta without sauce? Does it offer crayons and a paper placemat with a crossword puzzle, maze, and a word search to keep the kids occupied while we wait for our food?* Because if I want to have even five minutes to talk to my husband at the table, the kids need to be occupied. Period.

Even if, by some miracle, I can reach the ten-minute mark of chatter with other adults at the table, my kids will probably start arguing about who finished the word search or crossword puzzle first. There are sometimes tears, and maybe even a jab from one sibling to another.

This is why so many mothers tell me they don't go out to eat with their kids. It's not enjoyable to serve as referee and caregiver when you're trying to hold an adult conversation. Sure, there may be a few minutes where you think this time will be different. The kids will finally eat even half of their food (excluding the French fries), they will be kind to each other, they won't fight, they won't complain, they won't whine, they won't keep tapping you on the shoulder and say, "Mama, Mommy, Mami" until you respond, and then you realize—nope. Same shit. Your millisecond of hope is quickly interrupted with the reality that, yet again, going out to eat with kids can be stressful. You've accepted this reality. You've accepted that bringing children to a restaurant isn't going to be smooth sailing.

The only time it's not stressful is if we go to McDonald's. (Yes, my kids sometimes eat McDonald's; it's okay in moderation.) And it's not as stressful because we get Happy Meals to go.

So, why do we go out to eat with our kids? Because we want to feel like everyone else! We want to feel like "normal" adults, but if the kids come, I rarely can have an adult conversation. My young kids will interrupt until I respond (and it's not their fault; they want and deserve attention). Sometimes my three-year-old gets bold and calls me by my first name. That's when she's serious about getting attention.

With three little kids, going out to eat is not a calming or restorative time. And that's okay. It's not supposed to be. I refuse to raise robots under authoritarian rule who are taught that to "be good" means to be quiet, sit still, suppress discomfort and agitation, and don't question things or their parents. If engaging in more conscious parenting and providing my children with more freedom to express themselves (while still maintaining boundaries) means a more stressful dinner event, I'll take it. Of course, I'm simplifying this, but as mothers of young children, we accept that going out to eat isn't always going to be a peaceful experience. And if McDonald's is the only restaurant we can go to, so be it.

This is one of the many seasons of life, and it's the season I'm in. Knowing what season you're in makes it easier to navigate.

Monica Takes Stock

My client Monica came to me because she was at an inflection point. Six months prior to our meeting, her teenage son had been diagnosed with severe anxiety. Though she was an established executive, working on-site five days a week, nights, and weekends, too, she was considering her next move. She wanted to try her hand at a new challenge and a new company, and she knew she was not taking care of her health. Does this sound familiar?

Monica was in a season of caregiving for her son who needed daily attention. Her job didn't provide the flexibility to work remotely, and she needed to be at home. When we talked through how she would approach a new job, she knew herself well enough to know that, as an ambitious high achiever, she would continue to work hard and work late nights to get up to speed, add value in her position, and establish her reputation with new colleagues and leadership. She could already foresee how it would play out. Although she wanted a new challenge and a new job, Monica knew she would have to sacrifice the attention and care she wanted to give to her son.

Monica had a decision to make. She had to decide what was most important to her in this season. She needed a similar income to the one she was making, and she needed to have flexibility to be home. Yes, she wanted to do interesting work, but she recognized it was not the time to try something that would require more energy than she had to give. Monica ultimately decided to pursue a new job that was lateral in nature and remote so she could earn an income while caring for her son.

When I asked Monica what she would gain from this path, she said sanity, peace of mind, and a strong relationship with her son. In a different season in the future, she can lean into her career the way she'd like. This was not that season, and she recognized it.

Owning the season you're in, instead of continuing to harp on how life used to be or how it could be, gives you firm ground to stand on. When something unexpected happens, as it inevitably will, you won't be in reactive mode. The more you understand where you are in your life, the more you'll be able to make decisions and take actions in alignment with your priorities, values, and goals.

One of my favorite things about Monica, and the decision she made, is that she grabbed hold of Assessing where she was in her life, Assessing what her immediate priorities were, and then— with the full power of that knowledge—she was able to own it and Act accordingly. The work we did together to Assess her situation led directly to her making the necessary changes to accommodate her son's needs.

AWARENESS 101: THE WHEEL OF LIFE

How can you start the Assessment process? I got you. It all starts with a tool called the Wheel of Life, which is one of the most popular and effective psychology tools used in coaching.[1] Studies have shown that using the Wheel of Life leads to improved self-insight and awareness, self-esteem, and motivation to create positive change in your life.[2] It provides you with a bird's eye view of all the areas of your life, and it's a simple and effective way to Assess and identify the various areas of our lives that require our attention. Personally, I use it every three months, and many of my clients do the same. But this exercise can be repeated at a cadence that feels right to you. It's a tool you can throw into your live-your-best-life toolbox.

Once you're clear on what season of life you're in, the Wheel of Life provides further clarity by measuring your level of satisfaction across nine key areas. It's anchored in psychological research that says our well-being declines when we aren't in equilibrium, or when one or two areas of our life take a serious hit. Too much dissatisfaction in one area for too long can severely impact our overall state.

The Wheel of Life contains the following key areas for evaluation:

Now, give yourself a satisfaction rating for each
area on a scale of 1 to 10:
1 = I don't even want to talk about it!
10 = I'm on fire with this!

This is for you alone to see, so don't hold back. You might rate "love/partner" a five if you feel like you and your partner are ships passing in the night, if you feel like your relationship has become purely transactional, coordinating who picks up which kids when, and what the family plans are rather than finding space to connect with each other as partners.

After you write down your ratings, answer the following question in a journal (or wherever you'd like): *What are the reasons I rated each category this way?*

After you've written down your ratings and your reasons for each area, pick two—only two—with ratings on the lower end. Notice I didn't say pick your *lowest* ratings, because you need to be ready, willing, and able to create more satisfaction in the areas of your life of your choosing. Sometimes, picking an area with the lowest rating can feel overwhelming and sometimes not. It really depends on what you feel needs the most attention and focus during the specific season you're in.

> You need to be ready, willing, and able to create more satisfaction in the areas of your life of your choosing.

Once you pick your two areas, ask yourself the following questions:

- What's at stake if I don't improve my level of satisfaction in this area?

- How important are these things to me?
- What will I gain if I improve this area?

The key is to be honest. If you aren't honest in your assessment, it won't be helpful to you. It's for you and only you. This is a no-judgment zone and a no-criticism zone. You aren't allowed to temper or censor your satisfaction ratings with *but I should be so grateful* thoughts.

Let's assume you're grateful for every single experience that has led you to who you are and what you have today. Let's bask in our gratitude for a minute. I'm serious. Before you do the Wheel of Life exercise, think about (or better, write out) everything you're immensely grateful for. All of it. Then, do the exercise from that place. This way, you feel less guilty if you give an area of life a lower satisfaction rating.

The Wheel of Life helps you get honest with where you are and where you may need to focus to feel happier about your life and where you're headed. Feeling like our lives aren't as good as they could be, or getting used to a constant state of stress, exhaustion, or limbo is no way to live. You deserve to find joy. You deserve to feel peace. You deserve to find peace even as you work to increase the level of satisfaction in certain areas of your life. Doing the work and feeling at peace are not mutually exclusive. Just be open to believing more joy and fulfillment are possible for you.

So often, we don't see the window of opportunity, however small it seems, to pause and step off the treadmill of surviving to Assess how we're living. Identifying and accepting the season of life you're in and understanding where you'd like to put your intention and energy is a chance to be proactive about how you want to live your life and how you want to feel about it.

Tiffany Prioritizes Personal Time

Nearly out of breath, Tiffany turned to me and said, "I look to the future, and I don't want to be fifty-five years old and still feeling this way. I can't live like this anymore." For the past ten minutes, she shared why she came to me. Tiffany was in her early forties, a partner at a top law firm, working eighty-plus-hour weeks, sleeping barely six hours a night, and in her words, "had no time for herself." She loved hikes and walks in nature, but had no time for them anymore. She only saw her family twice a year and stayed for just a few days at a time, even though she adored them, especially her siblings, nieces, and nephews. She wanted to take longer than three days of vacation.

When I asked her what the most important area of her life was to focus on, she said personal life: time for herself, her family, and being with her friends. Translation, Tiffany was out of alignment with who she was and what she truly wanted and needed.

Whenever a client shares their story with me, it resonates every single time. I used to be each of them, in many ways. I've experienced firsthand the moment of reckoning: of reaching a breaking point, of realizing too much was at stake, and the cost was too high to not make a change. And, my friend, that moment is one indication you're ready and willing to do the work required to change your mindset from resignation to possibility and create lasting change in your life.

Tiffany was ready for change and willing to put in the work. She saw no other alternative. Looking ahead to her fifty-five-year-old self, she didn't like what she saw. Despite her schedule, which she described as hectic and chaotic, she committed to six months of coaching. When I told her she would be required to do pre-work before each session, she didn't skip a beat. She was "willing to do anything it takes." Game on.

Over the next six months, we worked through my 4-Part Framework.

1. Assess: Take stock of where you are.
2. Activate: Know your strengths, core values, and what gives you meaning and purpose.
3. Ask: What is your vision of your life in the future?
4. Align: Align your strengths, core values, priorities, and sense of meaning and purpose with your daily actions to bring you closer to your vision.

Starting with **Assess**, Tiffany and I identified what season of life she was in and her level of satisfaction within each area represented on the Wheel of Life: relationships (family and friends); love/partner; career/work; personal growth and learning; emotional, mental, and physical wellness; spirituality; finances; environment (work and home); and fun and recreation. I understood Tiffany came to me to focus on a personal life re-haul, but I knew the Wheel of Life exercise would help pinpoint other areas to be aware of. She scored the lowest in emotional, mental, and physical wellness; love/partner; personal growth and learning; relationships (family and friends);

and fun and recreation. These areas were all interrelated for Tiffany, and seeing her ratings gave her an understanding of where she really was at that point in her life: a season of professional acceleration and success, but at the sacrifice of her relationship with herself and the people she cared about most.

Moving into the **Activate** step, we delved into her strengths, values, and what gave her a sense of meaning and purpose in life. Tiffany loved her work, got paid well for it, and loved being the leader of her team. She was steadfast, confident, and diligent, and she cared deeply for the people she worked with and her family and friends.

One of Tiffany's core values was relationships, which played nicely into her strengths. But she had been neglecting the relationships that meant the most to her, including the one with her husband and her daughter. Tiffany also deeply valued giving back, and she wanted to mentor more of the junior women at her law firm. She wasn't doing as much as she wanted to, part of which was to clear the path for women and professionals of color to accelerate their growth and help support their professional advancement.

When I **Asked** Tiffany to share her vision for the future and articulate what she wanted her life to be like, her responses came quickly: freedom, joy, calmness, and time—time for herself, her family, friends, and time for the initiatives she cared about. We had to dig deeper into what that would actually look like for her. I walked Tiffany through a critical exercise, which led to a pivotal moment. It clarified what her future self needed at this moment to ensure she would not be in the same place in twenty years. (I'll share the exercise with you in Chapter 8: ASK.)

We then worked to **Align** her vision with her daily actions and decisions. Tiffany started small. To be clear, since Tiffany's self-assessment at the beginning of our time working together, we had been tweaking her daily habits to give her more time for herself in the morning. She had been blocking her calendar before 9 a.m., which turned out to be "Huge," she said. Previously, she took meetings and responded to emails starting at 6 a.m.! Every single morning, she made a choice to *not* go grab her laptop and gave herself alone time instead.

Inspired by the success of just one small change that led to huge results, we looked for ways to carve out more time. She started to take a twenty-minute break in the middle of her day to go for a walk outside. Next, we adjusted her bedtime routine. She was only getting six hours of sleep a night when we first met but she wanted to get nine to ten hours a night. At first, we set her bedtime at midnight, full stop. Over time, midnight slowly moved to 11 p.m., then 10 p.m., then 9:30 p.m. She even implemented a routine to wind herself down for bed by reading a book, rather than being on her laptop. In parallel, she was investing in more leisure time with herself, family, and friends. She started booking vacations—first, a solo trip, then a vacation with her group of girlfriends. Eventually, she booked trips to see her family across the country.

These are just some of the daily actions and deliberate decisions she made consistently over time that worked for her. But none of them would have been possible if Tiffany had not shifted her mindset to believe there was another way to live her life. She had to believe change was possible and be willing to try new things to see what worked and what didn't.

At first, she thought she was letting others down when she established boundaries with work. But then she remembered what was at stake if she continued to allow work to consume her life: time with herself to recharge and renew. Even when she was about to take a solo vacation or a trip to see family, she agonized over not taking her laptop. She thought of all the people who may need something from her, or work she needed to do. What would she do if she didn't have her laptop to do the work?

And then, with practice, she remembered—although work is important—spending quality time with herself or her family was *more* important. So, she learned to leave the dang laptop behind and felt a lot less guilt than before. She had committed to setting aside time to be with herself, and she stuck with it. She chose herself even when it was challenging to do so. She still does.

Monica and Tiffany devoted the time and energy to Assess, Activate, Ask, and Align their individual priorities, values, and purpose with their specific seasons of life. It's not easy to take a good hard look in the mirror and be honest with ourselves. The first crucial (and brave) step of Assessing where you are is how change begins to happen. I applaud Monica and Tiffany and the many other professional first-generation and women of color and mothers who have made the choice to step off the rollercoaster, Assess where their lives are heading, and work through the 4-Part Framework to embrace the possibility. If you're still with me, I'm betting you're one of those women. Stick with me; we're going places.

ACTIVATE: Your North Star

*"It's your road, and yours alone. Others may walk
it with you, but no one can walk it for you."*

—Rumi

After more than a decade of practicing law, I made the decision to say goodbye to the legal profession. To this day, some of my mentors don't fully understand why. They had been grooming me to be general counsel at a company, partner at a law firm, or a federal judge. They invested in me and connected me with other lawyers in the spaces I had once only dreamed I could occupy. When I told them I didn't want to be a lawyer anymore, they were confused and pushed back: "But you've worked so hard for this."

Had I, though? Years earlier, of course I had. If you knew me four or five years out of law school, I'd have you convinced I was going to be the first Latina federal judge in Massachusetts or a high-powered Latina partner crushing it at a large law firm. That was what I wanted at the time. It meant something to me to show my community, my family, and frankly—society—what we, as women of color, can accomplish, despite the obstacles we face. Any one of those positions would have represented the culmination of all my hard work. I genuinely believed then that with hard work, focus, determination, opportunity, support, and a sprinkling of luck, I would be able to do it. That was my truth, my vision, and my mission. But that was then.

THE INNER VOICE

What was I working so hard for *now*? I grappled with this question. If you think I was fed up with working the late nights and threw in the towel in frustration, you'd be mistaken. Not all lawyers hate their jobs, work around the clock, or have to put up with horrendous partners. Do you remember the story that went viral a few years ago of the partner who told a new mom associate she was "getting paid to do nothing" when she was on parental leave? Not many partners are like that. They may not totally respect all your boundaries because of the generally accepted notion that you get paid to work 24/7, but they aren't ill-intentioned. Not all lawyers are assholes. There are many lawyers who love what they do and how they do it.

At one point, I loved being a lawyer, too. I loved the "how" of my work: the research; writing; preparing oral arguments in front of a judge; collaborating on a team; the critical, analytical, and strategic thinking. Truthfully, I also loved what it afforded me. Growing up, I never even imagined what being a lawyer would be like, and becoming one exposed me to a whole new world. It made me feel important, like I'd "made it," and that felt really good. I also felt a little fancy. For the first time ever, I could buy myself whatever I wanted. I could travel all the time, and I did. It was so fun, and I felt free. But I also felt empty when I thought about the "what" of my work: the actual substance of the cases I worked on. Deep inside, I knew I wasn't wholly satisfied, but I just ignored the feeling.

If I'm honest, I felt this way long before I had my first child. I simply chose not to get curious about those feelings. I chose to stay focused on my work. I kept myself busy—which is another way we distract ourselves from facing the truth of our lives (although I was not aware of it at the time). But there was an inner tension, a little voice saying, "Do you really like this?" but I kept turning down the volume on that voice. I didn't engage with that question until after my son was born.

Birthing a tiny human changed me. It forced me to be with myself in a context outside of work. Although I didn't love the subject matter of my legal work, I missed the feeling of accomplishment from hitting deadlines, finishing a brief, filing a motion or an opposition to one, or analyzing the case law to make a helpful and critical point in an argument. I missed my source of validation.

Until that point, my self-worth was anchored to my accomplishments because, come hell or high water, I was going to make it. As the daughter of Dominican immigrant parents, I felt it was my job to prove their sacrifices were not in vain. They never told me to do this, but I felt it was my responsibility nonetheless. I chased success relentlessly, and how successful I appeared by capitalistic, societal standards was king.

What I had really been chasing was a feeling of enough-ness. All those years of grinding in school—from catching up to the grade level standards in high school to getting through law school and passing the bar—I was grinding for my worthiness, that I was good enough and smart enough, that I was worth something because of what I could accomplish despite the odds not being in my favor. Practicing law was an expression of not only the privilege and prestige of becoming a lawyer, but also what it took to get there. Looking back, I needed the grind to feel good. I was chasing that feeling that I could finally be proud of myself and take a break and breathe.

My sense of self and self-worth had been built on a foundation with deep, wide cracks.

Underneath all of my accomplishments was also a profound sadness because I knew I wasn't doing what I was put on this earth to do. My inner voice whispered—more loudly at times than others—that being a lawyer wasn't the way to make the large and positive impact I wanted to make, even though I was good at it.

> I knew I wasn't doing what I was put on this earth to do.

But here's the truth. I was making more money than I had ever seen in my life, and when you grow up without much money, financial security and stability become paramount. As a law firm lawyer, I was "successful" according to American societal standards and any immigrant parent. I was given credibility and respect because of it, and I can't say I didn't like it. I did. It made me feel special.

I was also terrified because, for years, I had ignored the calling for something else, while ignoring that my work didn't give me meaning. And I needed to feel more alive and fulfilled in my work. Not everyone does, and that's okay, but I did. Over six months of maternity leave, the realization that I wasn't fulfilling my true purpose crystallized, and I knew it wasn't going to happen at any law firm. Period.

A year after I returned from leave, I left the firm. I didn't immediately leave the legal profession behind (that would take four more years). But it was a massive step closer to who I knew I really was and what I had to start letting go of to find her. With two small children, a growing coaching practice, a weekly podcast, and a magnetic pull to help people grow and develop personally and professionally, I longed to Activate a more meaningful life for myself by better understanding my purpose, values, and strengths.

YOUR SENSE OF PURPOSE

Purpose is one of the strongest sources of grounding and motivation in your arsenal. Research shows resilience increases when you have a clear sense of purpose for why you're doing what you're doing. You're more likely to endure challenges and navigate them as opportunities for growth if they're aligned with your sense of purpose. You understand and have already bought into what's on the other side of the challenge.

A study in *The Journal of Positive Psychology* found that people who reported a strong sense of purpose were more likely to feel fulfilled and satisfied with their lives. Other studies have linked a sense of purpose to better mental health and longevity—more so even than factors like smoking, alcohol use, or exercise habits.[1]

For most people, and I know this was true for me, money is not the primary motivator. It's not even in the top three. In the 2018 World Economic Forum's Future of Jobs Report, meaningful work, work-life balance, and opportunities for growth and development were listed (in that order) as the most important for job satisfaction. Fair and competitive compensation was fifth.[2] Another study showed that employees who were motivated by a sense of meaning or purpose in their work were more likely to be engaged and committed to their jobs than those who were motivated by financial incentives.[3]

As the old adage goes, money can't buy happiness. Once your basic needs for comfort and security are met like food, clothing, shelter, and healthcare, more income does not necessarily lead to more happiness. As humans, we have the ability to adjust to new circumstances, which creates a new base level of happiness. Even the United Nations' World Happiness Report that analyzes happiness levels in countries around the world, found that while income is positively correlated with happiness, the relationship is not linear. There are diminishing returns beyond a certain income threshold. Making more money isn't going to magically make you leap into the bliss you think it will.

Let me be clear, money matters. That message rang loud and clear since I was young. I didn't have to be taught the value of a dollar. I saw it and experienced it. Money gives people access to more possibilities and opportunities for themselves and every subsequent generation. It provides access to a different lifestyle and resources like any type of education you'd want to provide for your children. But people who've hit certain income thresholds know that money isn't the silver bullet to feeling great about your life. Money is not determinative of happiness or the fulfill-ment you long to feel. A recent study found that having a lot of money is viewed as extremely or very important for a fulfilling life by less than a quarter of adults in the United States.[4] Money can improve certain aspects of your life, but once you adjust to that new baseline of more money, having more and more money doesn't matter as much as you think it does. And, what ends up happening is we continue to acquire more and do more—buy a bigger home, a nicer car, eat out more, go on more vacations—because our baseline keeps shifting. We forget that having all those material things is more about you and your feelings around what having those things mean. For some, it means they worked hard, and they earned it. Maybe they attach acquiring material things to their self-worth. For others, it's more about symboliz-ing to others, including their parents, that they made it.

Our purpose is to ignite who we truly are and step fully into liv-ing. So, I'll ask: What is your life purpose? Why are you here on this earth? If questions about your life's purpose cause a knot in your throat or give you hives, even for a millisecond, congratulations. You're a human being! Well-intentioned, personal development thought leaders ask you to figure out what you have been called to do and who you've been called to be on this earth. If you know the answer, you know your purpose. This characterization of purpose resonates with people who already know what theirs is.

But what if you don't know what your purpose is? What if you feel confused, lost, or simply like you're running on the treadmill of life without any grand "what" or "why" guiding you? I know how that feels, especially if you got on the treadmill and neglected to set the time or mileage goal. Because you didn't input your workout goal, the treadmill keeps going. It never shuts down. And here you are, still running on the damn treadmill. You're looking around to see if you're doing the right thing, as if someone else is going to come over and press the Off button, decrease your speed and incline, or pull the emergency tab. But no one is ever going to do that for you. No one is coming to save you. It's not that they don't want to. They probably do. But they can't do the thing that only you can do. Can you imagine being on the treadmill at the gym and someone came over to change your settings or your running goal? Nope. You want the power to decide when to speed up, when to slow down, and when to get off.

If that sounds like you, if you're looking for the decision-making power that will get you closer to your purpose, or if you've simply never thought about what your purpose is, that's okay. You've come to the right place.

Creating Space to Know Yourself

I'm the first to admit it's hard to set aside time so we may better understand and know ourselves. We haven't created the space or conserved the energy to allow for the type of self-exploration and reflection that reveals what we really think and feel. The more we practice creating the space to sit in what we think and feel, the closer we get to ourselves. It's the same as when you spend quality time with a friend. You get closer. You see them clearer. You connect with them more deeply. The better you know them, the more you're able to be there for them when they need your support and guidance.

The same is true for the relationship with yourself. When you spend time with yourself, you more deeply connect with all the different parts of you: the parts that terrify you, and the parts that excite you, and everything in between. You're more likely to see what you've been numbing, avoiding, and distracting yourself from. Spending more time with yourself is one way to start shedding all the outer layers and armor—like titles, accomplishments, and the checked boxes according to societal and cultural definitions of success—to get at what's underneath. And research shows that self-reflection combined with self-compassion promotes psychological well-being and fosters self-acceptance, resilience, and positive emotions.[5]

If you're reading this book, I hope you've found a quiet place to read it. What a gift! I don't know about you, but making the time to find a quiet space, even if it's at a café, which I find quieter than my home with three young children, has been a lifesaver for me. It's given me the ability to ask myself important questions and explore my answers from a place of honesty. It's given me the space to be curious and explore. This helps to uncover what I may be desperately avoiding or struggling with. I've come to better understand myself and what to do with what I think and feel. It's had the same impact on the women I work with, when they decide to do it and give it a chance. Are you ready to give it a shot?

Ask yourself

- What's my biggest challenge right now? What have I done to address it? What's at stake if I don't address it now?

- What do I really want right now in my life?

- What do I really need?

- What lights me up?

- Where am I holding myself back?

- What am I so afraid of or worried about?

- What (or who) am I avoiding?

Purpose is about igniting who you already are inside and living that part of you completely. It is intentionally amorphous, unfixed, and personal to you. I know what you might be thinking: *Wait, you're giving me a definition to tell me the definition depends on me?* Yes. Exactly.

Your sense of purpose can shift over time. What makes you feel lit up can shift and morph through the seasons, although the core of who you are often doesn't see massive shifts, even if you also have an overarching life purpose. And if you don't have an overarching life purpose? So what? You don't need one. Focus on what gives you a sense of purpose and meaning in *this season of your life*. For instance, you're ambitious and driven at work. What is the primary purpose of your job or work?

Let's make sure we differentiate between feeling a sense of purpose and significance. I'm sure you've heard that purpose is about being in service to others. Listen up, my friend: Purpose doesn't always need to be in service of others. That definition doesn't serve women, and especially not first-generation and women of color. We've been socialized to self-sacrifice like it's our job. So, I can't support adopting a definition of a word as powerful as purpose that reinforces a belief we need to unlearn. No thank you.

When you talk about serving others and making an impact on your community and the world, let's instead use the word *significance*. Significance is the deep desire to feel that you're making a difference in the lives of others and positively impacting them. Your goal to make a positive difference in others' lives motivates you to take risks and move through challenges. In his book, *The Dip: A Little Book That Teaches You When to Quit (and When to Stick)*, Seth Godin says the road to significance is not easy; it requires persistence, focus, and a willingness to push through difficult challenges. In this way, significance and purpose are closely linked, because they can both give you that extra push to navigate challenging seasons. But you don't have to be making a positive impact on others on a grand scale—which is significance—to have a sense of purpose or meaning in what you're doing in this season of your life.

Your sense of purpose or meaning may very well come from mothering your children, which, as you know, can feel like an invisible and thankless job at times. How you show up in your role as a mother isn't something that's visible to or immediately impacts a group or community. How you mother, however, has a massive, lasting impact on your children, and if applicable, your partner. So, mothering your children may not be your source for significance because it's missing that broader impact element, but it sure as hell gives you a sense of purpose and meaning.

As a professional badass, work may also be what gives you a sense of purpose and meaning. It may be what energizes you, or it may be what depletes you. Or, maybe there are parts you like and others you don't. You may have a feeling of dread every Sunday because you know Monday starts your crawl to Friday. You may not even get weekends off, because you're asked to do nonurgent work on the weekend with arbitrary deadlines. Cue the eye roll, please.

Even if you curse your job on the daily and feel it doesn't give you a sense of purpose, I'm going to bet that it *serves a specific purpose* in your current season of life. Maybe it helps you to provide for yourself and your family, to pay off your undergrad or graduate school loans, to fuel your three-month emergency fund, or to pay for your children's education. Maybe it helps you accumulate enough cash to make a down payment on a new home, and then maintain a monthly mortgage payment. Maybe it allows you to provide caregiving services for your parents, who need care that you're not physically able to provide, or to provide for your family. You see, dear reader, there are a plethora of reasons to work in a job you don't particularly like or feel ambivalent about.

The point is, simply by uncovering your sense of purpose—whatever it may be—you are Activating it. You are giving it the signal, "I see you. I know why I'm doing what I'm doing." This is a critical step in creating space to know yourself better and it empowers you to take ownership over your decisions.

Liliana Serves Her Purpose

For my client Liliana, her job was her number one nemesis. I don't typically use the word hate, but Liliana truly hated her consulting job. She hated being on call 24/7, responding to emails during dinner with friends, or having to be available to her more senior colleagues and partners at all hours. She hated having to cancel plans with her friends or her husband when a work matter required immediate attention. She said she was "so over it." Yet, she stayed for two more years. Why?

Even though Liliana hated her job and thought her colleagues were batshit crazy, she and her husband were saving to move out of their condo and buy a house with more space for their growing family. That was their plan. So, she stayed to make their dream happen. Her job served a specific purpose in her life: a home for her family. She decided to stop complaining about her job, and simply do it with her eyes on the prize. Two years later, Liliana and her husband bought a house. Her job helped make that happen for her family, and it was worth it.

You see, my friend, you're probably being too hard on yourself when it comes to the topic of purpose. People tend to think they need to have some grandiose life purpose. Focus instead of what gives you a *sense* of purpose and meaning. Ease up on the pressure you're putting on yourself to make yourself feel great about work all the time. It might not. And that's okay. Work can be part of a greater plan to help you reach a future goal. It doesn't always have to be as fulfilling as other aspects of your life. I'm giving you permission, if you need it, to let go of the pressure. Remember, your purpose is to live your life honestly and truthfully. It's to feel alive. It doesn't matter what form that takes, as long as you can feel the vitality in your bones, and as long as you are the one making the decisions for yourself.

Who Is Your Captain?

If you aren't being guided by the truest parts of you, something or someone else will guide you. Or you may be guided by what you think other people think of you. Either way, if *you* are not fully in charge of *you*, you're likely feeling some internal dissatisfaction and tension.

Don't relinquish control of your life or allow anyone else to be the captain of your ship. You're in charge of your own life, and though you may be influenced or driven by a variety of factors or people, your choices are yours to make.

> Your choices are yours to make.

Maybe the need for financial security is acting as the captain of your ship. Without truly defining what financial security looks like for you, you may feel that no amount of money will ever be enough. So, you keep working and keep earning. Your earnings increase over time, your lifestyle shifts, but you're still focused on creating the financial security and stability you may not have had growing up. If that's the case, chances are you never paused to think about what financial security and stability meant in actual dollars and lifestyle at this time in your life.

Or maybe the captain of your ship is an all too familiar beast: your parents, your family members, your community, or cultural expectations. How ironic is it that, even as grown-ass women, we're still scared of our parents in some way? We still feel the need to appease them, to not cause trouble, to not make a fuss. When we were children, being "good girls" was a strategy to stay out of the adults' way. We all did it, even our own parents. We were praised with this phrase when we did what we were told or when they were pleased with us. Children are smart. We deduced that if we didn't please our parents, we were bad and not worthy of their love. And as adults, we want to be "good" daughters. We don't want to cause our parents any pain. We certainly don't want to cause them worry or stress. They've undergone enough in life as it is. We never want to burden them, either as a child or as an adult.

What we can do, however, is decide when it's time to put our own stake in the ground. We can decide how to thoughtfully, kindly, and intentionally say what we need to say and do what we must do, even if it disappoints our parents or anyone else. I know this is easier said than done, and it's especially challenging for first-generation and women of color professionals, who often feel indebted to their parents and feel the weight of their families and communities to "succeed" in the traditional sense: get a college education, secure a stable and well-paying job, exhibit financial security, marry a "nice" person, have a few kids, buy a home, etc.

Well, what if you're reading this book and you don't actually want to have kids? What if you don't want to get married, either? What if you feel like you've made enough money to have the financial security you want? And what if you want to switch gears and do something else? What if you want to, for once—just once—follow a passion and see where it leads, instead of holding yourself back? Will your parents think you didn't appreciate their sacrifices or the lessons they taught you? Will you be letting them down? Sure, they'll worry about you. But that's what parents do, no matter how old you are. You know this well as a mother because you worry about your kids, too. You want them to make smart decisions and you know that there are decisions they'll make for them, that may not make as much sense to you.

Maybe your parents are not the captain of your ship though. Maybe the unspoken expectations of society at large have taken the helm of your life. Maybe it's not something anyone has said to you, but you still feel the weight of the expectations to drive your career at 100 mph, to be the primary caregiver as a mother, to exercise your face off, and to eat grain bowls to look like Jennifer Lopez or Kerry Washington. For the record, I love a grain bowl, especially with quinoa and sweet potatoes. I'm also a huge fan of Jennifer Lopez and Kerry Washington—who could forget the show *In Living Color* (J.Lo was a dancer before *Selena* and her career took off), and *Scandal* and *Little Fires Everywhere*. As a mother, you're often firing on all cylinders. And then you're told to make sure you're sleeping at least eight hours a night, taking hot baths for self-care, handling every birthday and activity for your kids, scheduling doctor's appointments, and managing all the other household and family duties. And there's this external pressure to make it look easy. Because good moms seem to make it look easy. They don't seem to outwardly struggle, and so you internalize this to mean that you can't break a sweat, either. You ask yourself: *How do they do this?*

Whichever or whoever's expectations you're trying to fulfill, they'll always keep you from feeling the sense of purpose and meaning you need to feel lit up inside because instead of disappointing them, you're disappointing yourself. Your spirit knows it. It's with you always, and you can't run from your spirit. You can't run from yourself.

> You can't run from your spirit.
> You can't run from yourself.

You are your own captain.

YOUR TRUE CORE VALUES

Your sense of purpose is the first of three critical pieces that Activate your North Star. It can help determine how you decide to behave and act each day. The second is your set of core values, which is the bedrock of what's most important to you and how you decide what to focus on in this season of life.

Core values and your sense of purpose are inextricably connected. For instance, my values of gratitude and life-long learning are closely aligned to what gives me a sense of purpose: personal growth and leveraging all I have to empower women, especially women of color, to rise up, to gain clarity, alignment, and fulfillment on their own terms.

Research shows that women who prioritize their core values tend to have a stronger sense of purpose and meaning in life and are more likely to engage in behaviors consistent with their values. This, in turn, leads to greater self-esteem and personal agency, which leads to improved mental health. That's not all. In studies conducted on the relationship between values and well-being, consistent findings revealed that knowing and living congruent with one's core values was associated with higher levels of life satisfaction.[6] Other studies show mindfulness and values-based actions and behaviors were significant predictors of well-being and life satisfaction.[7]

Women who prioritize intrinsic values such as personal growth, relationships, and contribution to community over extrinsic values such as wealth, titles, status, and appearance tend to be happier and more fulfilled.[8] Intrinsic values are more closely aligned with internal motivations and personal growth, while extrinsic values are often associated with external validations and comparison to others, which can be detrimental.[9] What is more, research shows that personal values related to being open to change (i.e., leaning into your own interests and desires) are positively correlated with well-being and that values focused on conservation (i.e., following the "rules," needing and seeking certainty, and preserving the status quo) are negatively correlated with well-being.[10]

Core values are the fundamental beliefs and principles that guide how you make decisions, how you live, and how you interact with others.[11] They don't change across situations. They represent what you care most deeply about, like freedom, family, well-being, honesty, or justice. You can have a long list of values to live by, but your core values are non-negotiable. They're the things you must adhere to no matter what. You know you're having an internal conflict of values when you feel tension, resistance, or friction in your body that you can't quite put your finger on. Your core values and vision (which we'll discuss in a bit) should align. That is, you should see your core values come through in your vision. If you didn't, it may be that you weren't as honest with yourself as you needed to be, or you censored yourself too much.

Marisol's Non-Negotiable

My client Marisol made the decision to leave an executive position primarily due to an attack on her core value of service. For Marisol, her job had to involve an element of serving the community. It didn't have to be her whole job, but it had to be part of her job. She had been leading community-based work at her firm and loved it. It gave her job meaning and it made all those long nights of answering work emails after the kids went to bed worth it. When she was asked to pull back on the desperately needed community initiatives she'd been leading, she tried to convince the firm's leadership of their importance. After months of meetings and futile attempts to save them, she finally had enough.

The firm's lack of support was a massive blow to how she felt about her work and herself. Marisol started to resent her job. It was a struggle to get through the day. Her work in the community was the main reason she'd stayed at the firm for the past five years. It was a pathway to fulfilling her values while doing her other billable work. For Marisol, the community-based work was just as important as the work that generated profit for the firm. The firm didn't see it that way.

Marisol's parents are immigrants, and they exemplified a strong work ethic and the importance of serving the community. Marisol deeply believed she could help others in her same position and wanted to blaze the trail for them. She worked tirelessly to receive her MBA and land a position at a top-ranked firm. She had always been involved in the community, serving on boards for nonprofit organizations, helping incoming first-generation college and MBA students with the transition to the undergraduate and graduate environments, and supporting first-generation professionals acclimate to the corporate environment with its unspoken expectations. Without that critical service component, Marisol's job no longer served her values, and she left.

Core values don't exist in a vacuum. They're deeply ingrained by our parents, upbringing, culture, and life experiences. If this is the first time you've taken the time to identify your core values, they may not scream at you like they did to Marisol. But if this is your first time reflecting on your core values, you should be damn proud of yourself. Many people don't ever carve out the time or space to get curious about what they stand for, what their beliefs and principles are, and how it impacts their decisions and behaviors. You're doing that right here, right now. Brava.

Values 101

Below is a three-part exercise I use with my coaching clients to help them get in touch with their core values. Let's dive in.

Part I: Get Curious

Write down your answers to the following questions in a journal or on your laptop, tablet, or phone. Writing them down gives you reflections to reference for the next part.

What does it look like when I show up as my best at work, with those I love and care about, and for myself? Be specific.

Example: What it looks like when I show up as my best.

1. At work, I'm collaborative and stay calm and kind under pressure. I am valued for my contributions and am viewed as a mentor to less-experienced colleagues.

2. With those I love and care about, I am compassionate. I listen closely and reserve judgment. My intent is to be supportive.

3. For myself, I'm consistently exercising during the week, carving out alone time each day (even if it's only fifteen minutes), and I'm eating food that nourishes my body. I'm dedicated to the hobbies that help me feel alive: playing the piano, drawing, and running.

What beliefs and principles guide your hardest decisions? Recall a time you made a hard decision (e.g., changing roles or jobs, moving homes, entering or ending a relationship) and use that to unpack this question.

Example: When I decided to move from legal and compliance to human resources, I had to confront the reality that I would not be practicing law anymore. I would be shedding a part of my identity. I was okay with that because I believe I was made for something different, something that being a lawyer could not fulfill.

Part II: Circle Ten Values That Resonate Most

With your Part I reflections in mind, review the following list of values. Circle ten values from the list that resonate most with you. You'll notice some of the values overlap with others. This is because wording and language are crucial. One word may not resonate as much as another (e.g., health versus well-being). Focus on choosing the wording that speaks to you. You need to be able to fully connect with and own your values, including how they are worded.

This is a non-exhaustive list. It would not be possible to include every single value for all humans, but these are the ones I've seen come up the most.

- Love
- Gratitude
- Joy
- Truth
- Kindness
- Hope
- Compassion
- Service
- Community
- Teaching
- Learning
- Curiosity
- Openness
- Growth
- Humility
- Authenticity
- Courage
- Collaboration
- Perseverance
- Achievement
- Ambition
- Leadership
- Personal fulfillment
- Career
- Excellence
- Success
- Loyalty
- Confidence

- Honesty
- Forgiveness
- Wisdom
- Trust
- Integrity
- Reliability
- Responsibility
- Respect
- Belonging
- Diversity
- Inclusion
- Dignity
- Future generations
- Equity
- Fairness
- Justice
- Creativity
- Independence
- Efficiency
- Environment
- Family
- Parenting
- Giving back
- Freedom
- Patience
- Spirituality
- Generosity
- Self-love

- Humor
- Fun
- Understanding
- Vulnerability
- Health
- Optimism
- Financial stability
- Job security
- Making a difference
- Recognition
- Legacy
- Self-expression
- Culture
- Power
- Knowledge
- Order
- Organization
- Well-being
- Wealth
- Travel
- Time
- Friendship
- Peace
- Faith
- Contribution
- Significance
- Nature
- Caring

Review the ten values you circled. How do you feel about them? If the values you circled seem aligned with your beliefs and priorities, move on to the next step. If they don't, look at the list one more time and make changes. No ruminating, though, my friend. Move on to the next step to keep your momentum with the exercise.

Part III: Cull Your List to Five Values

To narrow down your list to five values (bonus if you can get them to three to sharpen your clarity even more) ask yourself:

- How do *I* define each of the values I selected?

- Are the definitions similar? For instance, the values of learning and growth seem similar but do they have different meanings? If they are very similar, pick one of the two by considering which word makes you feel more expansive than the other. Language is powerful: The word you choose must mirror how you feel inside.

- Are these values truly *mine* or do they represent what is expected of me? There is no judgment here. No one is going to look at your list. This is for your own self-awareness and exploration.

- Do these values define who I am, even if I'm not fully aligned with them in this season? If you're in the thick of being a mom of toddlers, you're probably simultaneously accelerating in your career. You might be working late after you put the kids to bed. You might get up earlier than your kids to exercise or work. You might feel guilty for working on the weekends and not spending that time with them or on yourself (no work, no kids, just you). Your behavior today doesn't mean you don't value parenting and family. There's no singular way to behave to live the values of parenting and family. I only ask that you consider if you're living in congruence with how *you* define that value and make it real.

You may certainly have ten or more values that resonate, but all ten are not your *core* values. Narrowing down to core values helps you get crystal clear on what is most important. If everything is important to you, nothing is important because you'll continue to be pulled in multiple different directions at the same time. You'll continue to play whack-a-mole. You continue to say yes, when you mean to say no. You won't set or enforce the boundaries that will help you feel more peace and freedom and less stress.

When you're clear about your core values, you'll make better decisions that align with your beliefs. You'll be able to prioritize your goals and the things that bring you joy and fulfillment—the things that lead to more sanity and less chaos—in this season. You're less likely to be lured by distractions or temporary emotions that pull you away from what's most important. You'll know how to focus your time, energy, and resources on the people and activities that matter most. You become more confident that you're living life authentically and with integrity, even when you're navigating difficult life decisions and coping with stress.[12]

YOUR STRENGTHS, YOUR POWER

Your strengths make up the third critical piece to Activate your North Star. Focusing on your strengths forces you to turn your attention to what's going well and what you're doing right, instead of what's going wrong.

You'll often hear that therapy takes a client from nonfunctioning to baseline, and coaching takes a client from baseline to flourishing. There's a reason coaches use this terminology. The phrase "human flourishing" was coined by the founder of positive psychology, Martin Seligman. Essentially, it means experiencing high levels of social, mental, emotional, and physical well-being.

According to Seligman's research, there are five central elements of human flourishing: positive emotions, engagement, relationships, meaning, and accomplishment. Further, he identified twenty-four character strengths that underpin these elements, which are now well known as the VIA character strengths. These strengths include creativity, bravery, kindness, perspective, curiosity, fairness, leadership, perseverance, teamwork, appreciation of beauty, and excellence, among others. Seligman found that exercising "your highest strengths leads to more positive emotions, to more meaning, to more accomplishments, and to better relationships."[13] In other words, it improves your well-being and your life satisfaction.

Strengths Assessment 101

Give yourself thirty minutes to take Seligman's evidence-based VIA strengths assessment, which can be found at https://www.viacharacter.org/. Focus on your top five strengths and look at how they are showing up, or not showing up, in your life.

Evidence-based strengths assessments, rooted in positive psychology, can be deeply impactful for high-achieving professional women. A strengths assessment helps you see what's amazing about who you already are. It's not about what's wrong with you (and nothing is wrong with you, by the way). You probably spend enough time punishing yourself for not fulfilling all the roles you play with perfection, even though you logically understand perfection doesn't exist. The strengths assessment is a reminder to double down on your talents and pay less attention to your negative self-talk. Knowing your strengths also provides a window into the reason you feel tension and friction in your job or other areas of your life, because tension intensifies when you aren't exercising your personal strengths and you feel misaligned.

Carolina Takes the Ball

My client Carolina came to me because she was feeling unsatisfied with her job. She had put in nearly twelve years at her company. After several promotions, she'd been in her current position for about three years. The last year had been particularly challenging because she started to feel ambivalent about her work and was more easily frustrated with it. She felt isolated and wanted more autonomy and responsibility over a larger team, and she wanted recognition for her contributions and hard work, as she justly earned and deserved.

I asked Carolina to take the VIA character strengths assessment. I've witnessed many a-ha moments for my clients when they've taken this assessment. And sure enough, a light bulb went off for Carolina when we reviewed her results. Two of her top five strengths were fairness and leadership. She wasn't able to exercise either of those strengths in her current position in the way she wanted, and she was not sure if she would ever be able to.

Although she spoke casually about leaving her job, after she took the strengths assessment and saw herself reflected in the results, she began to seriously consider it.

The exercise generated just the right amount of introspection to motivate her to explore two viable options: one, leave for another opportunity where she could more fully exercise her strengths, or two, ask for an expanded role at her company. She bravely chose to ask for more. The higher-ups said she would have to wait a few years.

The ball was in Carolina's hands. When she thought about leaving and going elsewhere, fear crept in. She was afraid of the unknown, worried about how she would do with a new manager and colleagues, whether she could build her reputation with new people again. She didn't want to start over again and have to prove herself in a new environment after she had already devoted twelve years to her current company.

We talked through her values, strengths, and what she wanted most at this time in her life. Carolina was clear that her situation had become untenable. She wanted more. I had to hold up a mirror so she could fully see and appreciate the evidence that as a high achiever and performer, she had everything she needed to crush any job she took on. She had to accept not knowing how it would all turn out, while also trusting she could navigate whatever happened moving forward.

And Carolina was done waiting. She leaned into her fear and doubts, trusted herself, and left the company. One year later, she was in a higher position at a new job. And she was able to fully rely on her strengths as the leader of a larger team.

I'm going to let you in on a secret. Do you know what *value* rose to the very top when Carolina did her three-part exercise? You guessed it: leadership. This was not a coincidence. Just as your values are inextricably linked to your sense of purpose, values are also connected to your strengths. For example, "learning" is one of my top three values and it's also a top three strength. Learning is what has given me a sense of purpose in every job I've ever had. If I'm learning and growing, I feel energized and motivated. Again, this isn't a coincidence.

I'm asking you to do these exercises across purpose, values, and strengths so you can experience the overlap between them and stop second-guessing yourself. The point is to unlock, reinforce, and Activate what you already know deep down inside.

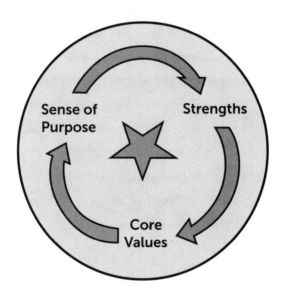

Together, your sense of purpose, core values, and strengths form your North Star. They provide the framework to decide what your actions and priorities will be in this season. Your North Star is the lens through which you consider life and career decisions. It's your anchor and your guiding light. When in doubt, your North Star is one of the most powerful tools to bring you back to yourself and what matters most. It also serves as a foundation as you consider what life could look like in one, five, or ten years. And by what life could look like, I mean what a great, joyful, aligned life could look like—yes, even in the season of motherhood!

ASK: Create Your Vision

"If you don't like the way your life is going, redesign it. Redeem the years you lost. Restore your vision, revive your passion for living, and reclaim what was dormant inside of you."

—T. D. Jakes

Nina paused along the light stone pathway that led to the front door of a cream-colored stucco house. It was nestled amid the lushest greenery she'd ever seen. She took a moment to notice it—to really notice it—and she breathed in the serenity surrounding her. Nina slowly continued up the pathway to reach the front door, let out a big exhale, and knocked, anxious to see who would be home to greet her.

A woman twenty years older answered the door. Nina noticed the woman's gold hoop earrings behind her curly dark brown hair, her pale blue linen dress, and her bare feet. Nina couldn't remember the last time she was barefoot in her own house. She was always on her way somewhere, either driving her teenage son around or taking care of the gazillion things she needed to deal with as the default primary caregiver and household manager.

Nina noticed how calm and warm the woman was as she welcomed her inside. Following the woman farther into the house over clean, white tiled floors, there were fresh plants placed elegantly along the corridor and the white walls were covered in artwork, which Nina was sure had been collected from different parts of the world. Nina loved traveling and had built up her own small but mighty art collection from her trips. There was not a single TV, laptop, tablet, or phone in sight. As she walked through the house to the back patio, a sense of ease came over her. There was no distraction here, nothing to "get done," nothing to keep her busy. Nina realized she had not felt this at ease in years.

The woman sat down in one of two chairs, invited Nina to sit in the other one, and asked the reason for her visit. Nina wanted to know what the woman's life was like. The woman smiled and explained she was free to work wherever she wanted. She had retired a few years earlier but continued to work intermittently for certain clients because she loved it. Her family and friends often came to visit, and she visited them, too. Nina found herself staring at the woman as she spoke, and felt her calm energy. She felt at peace listening to her talk.

Nina asked the woman what she needed to know or change to feel the same type of freedom, calm, and happiness. The woman's answer was simple: "Prioritize yourself and your personal life over work, because work never prioritizes you. When the work hustle is over, you'll be left with yourself and your relationships. If you haven't taken care of yourself or your relationships, you'll have nothing, and it could be too late. Focus on what will really matter to you in the end."

This resonated. Nina had been working nonstop and taking care of her teenage son; she spent most of her time going to networking events and conferences with clients and colleagues. But she had not spent quality time with friends and family on a consistent basis in years. When she visited her family, she only stayed a night or two. She used to take trips with friends, but that ended when her son was born fourteen years earlier.

The woman told Nina to stop waiting and take control of her life now. She reminded Nina she was more than capable of doing it; she simply had to decide it was time. As the conversation came to its natural conclusion, Nina thanked the woman for her guidance. They shared a warm, long embrace before Nina left. As she walked down the pathway away from the house, Nina was hopeful she would be like that woman in twenty years.

This interaction was the result of a visualization exercise Nina and I did together. The woman in Nina's story is herself in twenty years. I Asked Nina to envision her future, and after utilizing the tools she Activated in our previous work together—her purpose, her core values, and her strengths—she was able to anchor to a future version of herself. To this day, Nina says it was one of the most powerful exercises she has ever done. It continues to inform how she shows up for herself and those she cares for the most every day, and it reminds her of what is most important in her life.

WHY HAVING A VISION MATTERS

Why is Asking someone (or asking yourself) to articulate a vision for the future so necessary? Allow me to channel Iyanla Vanzant,

a motivational speaker, author, spiritual teacher, and former lawyer. When I saw her speak live over five years ago, I remember
feeling the energy that emanated from her, 200 feet away, in a
room of more than 5,000 women lawyers of color. Her words were
a mixture of warmth, love, kindness, and a swift kick in the ass.

She said, "If you don't have a vision, you're going to be stuck
in what you know. And the only thing you know is what you've
already seen. But a vision that grows inside of you—a bastion that
wakes with you, sleeps with you, moves with you—a vision that you
can tap into on your worst days . . . that vision pulls you forward."

Iyanla focuses on helping women grow and heal. She and I
agree that personal growth and healing require having a vision,
which is one of the most underestimated and underutilized tools
you can leverage to figure out where you need to focus your attention right now to create your future.

Visualization, or envisioning one's future, is a technique that
involves creating guided or mental imagery to enhance your
focus and belief in achieving your goals. It's a process of using
your imagination to form a clear and detailed mental representation of specific desires and outcomes. It's an opportunity for
what lies dormant in your subconscious mind to come forward
into your conscious mind. Manifestation, on the other hand, is a
broader concept extending beyond visualization. Manifestation is
the belief that intentions and thoughts can influence the external
world and create the outcomes we want. Manifestation typically
involves gratitude practices, visualization, mindset shifts, positive
affirmations, and taking action to reach your goals. Manifestation
can certainly involve visualization but is not limited to it.

The research on visualization has focused on its impact on how we function as humans—namely, performance enhancement, goal achievement, and mental and emotional well-being. You may have heard of professional athletes visualizing themselves successfully performing a skill that improves their performance in real time when it counts the most. Stephen Curry from the Golden State Warriors, and arguably the best three-point shooter in the NBA, has leveraged visualization to improve his game-time performance when his team relies on him to make his famous three-point shots in the last few seconds of a game to win. Studies have also shown visualization helps athletes increase their persistence and motivation to reach their goals.

Visioning exercises help you gain clarity about what you really want and need, and the direction you need to move in to get it. When you visualize the future, you can use it as a filter to ensure your decisions align with moving closer in that direction. You're better able to focus attention in that direction and are less likely to be distracted by shiny things that lead you down dead ends or detours.

Visualizing the future in a general way is powerful. But there's an even more effective approach: episodic future thinking (EFT), a thought process that creates a mental representation, imagination, or simulation of a future event. In the past two decades, there have been around 5,000 peer-reviewed scientific studies on EFT. When we construct a mental image of ourselves in a particular location, at a particular time in the future, we simulate more specific and detailed futures. This process allows us to anticipate possible outcomes of our actions from a more objective perspective.[1]

The more time you place between today and your future event, the more likely you are to see the person in that future as separate from who you are now. EFT researchers refer to this as viewing yourself in the third person rather than the first person. That is, you are less attached to your ego and who you are today, and you can detach from your current thoughts and fears, which can be limiting. You are less likely to get caught up in your existing to-dos and how they impact you, because you're creating distance between the person you are now and the person you envision being in the future.

Visualization leads to a tangible and concrete idea of what you want out of your life and your essential needs. You're creating a vivid mental story and image in your mind and a physical experience in your body. You're using all your senses to see, smell, taste, hear, and touch the future experience. Many women say they'd like freedom, peace, joy, aliveness, fulfillment, work-life integration, and alignment in their lives. By visualizing a specific time in your future, you get to define what those words mean in your future life.

For Nina, the visioning exercise shined a light on who she *could* be, and the work to become that person began immediately. She was so excited by what she saw, she was no longer willing to delay the actions necessary to get there until a faraway future date. Nina had to decide how to prioritize herself in the busy season of her life as an executive, leading a consulting practice, and the parent of a teenager. To do that, we started small and focused on each goal and each step until she finally found her work-personal life integration in the optimal place. All she had to do then was maintain what she had created for herself.

LOOKING BACK TO LOOK AHEAD

Let's start priming our minds for the future by looking backward. You might be asking: *Why are we looking backward, when we're focusing forward?* A-ha. Sometimes we need to look backward to appreciate the present and to anticipate the road ahead. Healing work often requires that we dig into our past to uncover thought patterns and beliefs that may have served us at one point, but no longer do.

For example, I know you have high standards and expectations, and when you don't meet them, you might punish yourself by ruminating on a misstep, by telling yourself that something must be wrong with you, or that you don't deserve to be where you are, or worse. I'm not suggesting you lower your high standards or to let go of your drive and ambition. Drive, ambition, and standards of excellence—typical perfectionist traits—are not inherently unhealthy.

Katherine Morgan Schafler is a psychotherapist to high-achieving women lawyers and executives on Wall Street talks about this very thing. In her book, *The Perfectionist's Guide to Losing Control: A Path to Peace and Power*, she shares some startling news: Perfectionism is not always a bad thing, but she also delineates between adaptive and maladaptive perfectionism. Adaptive perfectionist standards of excellence can serve you well as a strength to be celebrated. Yes, I too let out a big sigh of relief when I learned this. But when they are maladaptive, they can make you feel like shit.

Adaptive perfectionists own their self-worth and are driven by achieving goals they set for themselves. They are ambitious, and when they make a mistake, they do not internalize it or use it as evidence of failure. Maladaptive perfectionists, on the other hand, are chronic self-punishers and experience shame, fear, and feelings of failure when they make a mistake. They beat themselves up way too much, and they rely on approval from others to feel worthy. Their best effort is never good enough because they fear imperfection (despite knowing that 100 percent perfection does not exist). Their success is driven by the need to avoid failure.

Does this sound like you? If so, you'll want to take a step back and notice how you're talking to and treating yourself, and reframe those thoughts so they lift you up rather than tear you down.

Self-Appreciation 101

Regardless of whether you resonate more with adaptive or maladaptive types of perfectionism, or have a mixture of both, the following exercise will allow you to see that you have so much to be proud of. It will help you press Pause on the spinning thoughts in your mind, telling you that what you've done is not enough or good enough.

Think back to ten years ago.

Choose a specific moment and place from that time of your life.

- Where were you?
- Who were you with, if anyone?
- What were you doing, wearing, and seeing?
- If you have kids now, did you have them then?
- What was going on in your career?

- What were you excited about?

- What were you worried about?

- What fears did you have?

- What challenges were you navigating?

- Were you working toward a life or career goal?

- What has changed in your life the most since then?

Now, write down three things that are true about your life today that would have surprised you ten years ago. Go ahead, write it in the margins if you want. Just write it down somewhere.

The purpose of this exercise is to take a good, hard look at how many things have changed, how much you've transformed, and how far you've come. We often don't see how much we're evolving as we're evolving. Even if we do, we aren't able to see the extent of the evolution, unless we create some distance and view it from a different vantage point. We don't do this often enough.

Notice, the missteps or mistakes you made in the past didn't render you a failure. On the contrary, you rose above each challenge. You navigated difficult times, including the times you didn't know how you'd make it through.

Every single experience you've had has led you to this moment right now, reading the words in this sentence, choosing to Assess, Activate, Ask,

> Every single experience you've had has led you to this moment right now.

and Align your priorities, strengths, purpose, and values with your current season of your life and your vision for the future.

Sit with this for a minute. Recognize how far you've come, my love, and bask in it. All of it. You deserve to do this for yourself. We were conditioned not to sink into the cushion of our thrones when we experienced a success. Why? For two main reasons: one, you were expected to do well and experience success after success, and two, you're always striving for the next thing, to the degree you don't stop to recognize and appreciate the thing you just did. I'm asking you to bring attention to that conditioning and start shedding it, so you can give the gift of celebration to yourself.

FUTURE THINKING IN PRACTICE

Now that you've successfully reminded your brain of all you've been able to navigate and become in the past decade, let's turn our attention to the future.

The following three exercises are based on research-validated EFT methodology, which will help you move beyond what is directly in front of you today, create a different vantage point, and give you the mental space to think about the future.

I encourage you to try each exercise because they offer different benefits, and I recommend following the order in which they are presented here: one year, ten year, and then twenty year. If you only choose one, go for the twenty-year exercise to lock into your future self. All three exercises are available in audio format for download here.

One-Year Visioning: https://www.ariveevargas.com/book

Ten-Year Visioning: https://www.ariveevargas.com/book

Twenty-Year Visioning: https://www.ariveevargas.com/book

Give yourself at least three days in between each exercise for reflection.

This is how each visioning exercise works.

1. Find a quiet, physical space that feels expansive, like a room with a lot of natural light, a park bench, or somewhere outside, and/or by a body of water. The right environment will help open up your senses and your mind for the visioning exercise.

2. Ensure you won't be interrupted. Make sure your children are attended to, your schedule is clear, and your phone is silenced.

3. Read (or listen) to the prompt for the appropriate visioning exercise all the way through.

4. Relax, close your eyes, and focus deeply on the instructions in the prompt.

5. Write down what you saw in your mind.

Why do you need to write it down? Isn't it enough to envision what you saw in your mind? The short answer is no. The longer answer is scientific studies have shown that your brain will place a higher importance on something and remember it better if it is written down[2] because handwriting promotes deeper cognitive processing.[3] One study showed that students who took notes by hand were more likely to remember and prioritize important information compared to those who used laptops.[4] Thus, writing your vision down sends a signal to your brain that it's important and deserves increased attention and focus.

With these instructions in mind, read or listen to each of the following.

The One-Year Vision

Find a comfortable position and close your eyes. Take five deep breaths using box breathing: Inhale for four seconds, hold for four seconds, exhale for four seconds, and hold for four seconds. Repeat five times.

This will help calm your nervous system and take you into the present moment. You're now breathing normally. Relax your mouth and release any clenching of your teeth or jaw.

Let your hands simply fall where they are. If you are lying

down, maybe they are resting on your hips, belly, or the material you're lying on. If you are sitting, keep your hands relaxed on your thighs.

Continue breathing in and out.

You are feeling more at ease. You are feeling more relaxed.

We're going to move into the one-year visioning exercise now.

You and I have been planning to get together for a year now. We finally scheduled it, and it's happening. We decide to meet at a café for lunch. I arrive early and grab a table. Sitting at our table, I notice you walk into the café. I wave and you start walking over. As you get closer, I immediately notice the way you're taking up space. You have a powerful presence. I'm talking Beyoncé presence vibes. You're glowing, and there is something radiating from inside of you. I can feel it.

I get up from my seat and say, "Oh my gosh, it's been too long!" as we give each other a long, tight hug, the kind that says more than words ever can. I loosen my grip on you, but I'm still holding your arms with my hands, and I ask, "How are you?!"

We sit down. With eyes wide open, as if you cannot believe what you're about to share, you say, "This has been the best year of my life."

I'm so excited for you, and want to know more, so I ask, "That's amazing. I'm so happy for you. What made this past year the best one ever? I need all the details."

You walk me through what has happened in all the different areas of your life over the past year: work or career, finances, relationships, wellness and self-care routines, lessons learned, and the big and small changes. As you're sharing with me, you recognize how far you've come and how much you've grown.

You say, "I can't believe it, but I'm doing it."

Now, write down everything you shared with me. Take your time.

As you write, remember:

- Check in with your heart.

- Are you being honest with yourself?

- Are you telling yourself stories to diminish your own vision for your life?

- If you're telling yourself this can't work, ask yourself instead: *How can I make it work? What would happen if it does work out? What is the worst that can happen and the best that can happen?*

The Ten-Year Vision

Before we get into the ten-year visioning exercise, you might find it interesting to know scientific research shows that the ten-year time frame provides enough temporal distance to lead to more expansive and ambitious goal setting.[5] A ten-year timeline makes us feel like we have time to learn, grow, and figure out how to reach our goals. What we can envision accomplishing in ten years feels less daunting because it's far enough away that we don't feel pressure to reach all our goals now. And our brains respond positively to the abundance of a ten-year period.

Think of the looking-back exercise you did in the previous section and how much your life has changed in the past ten years. The next ten years will see similar levels of change—some things will happen to you and other things will happen because you made them happen. You don't have control over the things that will happen to you, necessarily, but you can intentionally and thoughtfully decide what you'll make happen in the next ten years. Think vividly about what is plausible in that time frame.

Don't get me wrong. This isn't the same as asking: If you could wave a magic wand and had endless resources, what would you do with your life? I love this question because it can bring forward insights about things you may want to do that you've been subconsciously suppressing or avoiding. Of course, I believe you have the determination, drive, willpower, and ability to achieve any of your goals. But I'm not asking you to focus only on your achievements or accomplishments. This is about how you see the *person you'll be* in ten years. I dream of headlining for Beyoncé, but that's not where I'm going to focus my future visioning. I'd rather focus my brain on the future I actually see for myself and the kind of life I want to lead.

With that in mind, let's get started.

Find a comfortable position and close your eyes. Take five deep breaths using box breathing: Inhale for four seconds, hold for four seconds, exhale for four seconds, and hold for four seconds. Repeat this five times.

Release what's in front of you for the rest of the day. Say the word "release" out loud eight times: "Release. Release. Release. Release. Release. Release. Release. Release."

Feel the tension release from your body.

Relax your mouth and release any clenching of your teeth or jaw.

Let your hands simply fall where they are. Maybe they are resting on your hips, belly, or the material you're lying on.

You are feeling more at ease now. You are feeling more relaxed. Keep your eyes closed.

Imagine you wake up one Monday morning ten years from now. You've woken up naturally, without the alarm.

- Where are you? Are you in your bed or somewhere else?

- Look around and notice your surroundings.

- What does the room look like?

- Is anyone next to you?

- What do you hear?

- What do you smell?

- Is sunlight beaming through the windows or is the room dark?

- When you place your feet on the floor as you get out of the bed, what do you do first?

- How will you spend your time today?

- What is most important to you in terms of how you spend your time?

- Who is in your life and not in your life anymore?

- What do you really want in this future moment and what are you working on?

Take the time to envision it. Breathe in that vision. Hold it there.

Now, open your eyes. Write down what you saw.

Next, write down your answers to these questions:

- How do you feel, now that you're here, ten years into the future?

- What is true about this life in ten years that is not true today?

- What has changed the most in ten years?

When you're writing, remember:

- Check in with your heart.

- Are you being honest with yourself?

- Are you telling yourself stories to diminish your own vision for your life?

- If you are stuck on how your vision won't work out, consider: *what would happen if it does? What's the worst that can happen and the best that can happen?*

The Twenty-Year Vision

Just as Nina did at the beginning of this chapter, you're now going to meet yourself in twenty years. If you're thinking this is a long time, you're right. That's the point. Twenty years gives your brain the freedom to imagine a new future reality that may be light years from your current one. It gives your mind permission to run wild and free. Allow it to run as wild and free as it wants. Let's begin.

Find a comfortable position, and close your eyes. Take five deep breaths using box breathing: Inhale for four seconds, hold for four seconds, exhale for four seconds, and hold for four seconds. Repeat this five times.

Release what's in front of you for the rest of the day. Say the word "release" out loud eight times: "Release. Release. Release. Release. Release. Release. Release. Release."

Feel the tension release from your body.

Relax your mouth and release any clenching of your teeth or jaw. Let your hands simply fall where they are. Maybe they are resting on your hips, belly, or the material you're lying on.

You are feeling more at ease now. You are feeling more relaxed.

Now, put yourself in the car. You've had a long drive. You step out of the car and your feet land on the driveway beneath you. As you get out of the car, you look up and take in what you see. There's a house about thirty feet in front of you.

- What surrounds you as you stand next to the car and look around?
- What does the house look like?
- What color is it?
- What style of house is it?
- What surrounds the house?
- What do you see in the distance?
- Is there anyone around you?
- What do you hear?
- What do you smell?

You see there's a stone pathway leading to the front of the house. You take another minute to look around. You breathe in the air a few times to ground yourself in this moment. You start on the pathway to the house. You take one step and then another. You're walking slowly, not because you are hesitant to reach the house, but because you are still looking around at the surroundings. You're taking it all in. Take it all in.

You finally reach the door, and you notice there isn't a doorbell, so you knock a few times. After a minute or so, you hear someone's footsteps approaching the door.

A woman twenty years older than you opens the door. She smiles as she greets you.

- What does she say to you?
- What do you say in response?
- What does she look like?
- Take in every detail: her hair color and style, her clothes, her shoes if she is wearing any, and her jewelry if she's wearing any.
- How do you feel as you take her in?

She welcomes you into the house and asks you to follow her to a seating area on the back patio that has two chairs.

- What do you notice about her presence and how she's walking with you?
- What is she saying to you as you follow her?
- What do you notice inside of the house as you're heading to the seating area?
- What does the furniture look like?
- What is on the walls?
- Do you see any electronics; if so, what do you see?
- Do you see anyone else in the house; if so, who?

You reach the patio where the woman invites you to take a seat. You are sitting next to each other, but you have turned your bodies to face each other. You don't speak right away. You look at her more closely now. You notice her face and the life in it. If her presence didn't strike you before, it does now.

- What do you notice about her now that you're closer, face-to-face?

The woman asks what she can help you with and if you have any questions for her. You thought she'd never ask; you want to know so much about her! You start asking her a series of questions. Take the time to really process her answers.

Ask her:

- What her life is like. Listen intently. She's sharing the details of her daily life with you.

- What the past twenty years have been like, and please do not spare any details.

- How the kids are, if you chose to have them.

- Who have they become?

- Who does she spend time with? Listen for who she spends the most time with.

- What she does for herself each day?

- What is she sharing with you?

Notice how you feel when you hear her answers. Notice the energy between you two and the energy she exudes.

Now, ask her:

- What do you need to know about how you're living your life right now?

- Does she have any advice about how you can experience more joy and fulfillment?

- Does she have advice about how to feel more of what you want to feel and less of what you don't?

- What do you need to do differently to live the life you want?

Here, she pauses. She looks at you as if she sees through you, and asks: "Well, what is the life you want to lead? Who do you want to become in living it?"

Take a minute to think how you'll answer her. When you're ready, share your answer with her. What is her response to you?

As the conversation comes to its natural conclusion, you thank the woman for her guidance, and you share a warm, long embrace before you turn around to leave. As you walk down the pathway from the house, how do you feel? What thoughts come to mind as you get into your car to drive back home?

Now, write down every detail you can remember about what you saw in your mind and the interaction between you and the woman.

Be sure to include:

- What is true about this life in twenty years that is not true today?

- What has changed the most in twenty years?

- How did it feel to meet the twenty-year-older version of you?

- What about what she said resonated the most with you?

- What about the experience with her surprised you the most?

Remember:

- Check in with your heart.
- Are you being honest with yourself?
- Are you telling yourself stories to diminish your own vision for your life?

If you are stuck on how your vision won't work out, consider: *what would happen if it does work out? What's the worst that can happen and the best that can happen?*

How to Use Your Vision Write-Ups

First, congratulations on completing at least one of the future visioning exercises! Most people don't give themselves the space to think about their future in a vivid and plausible way. You've done that, and you should be damn proud of yourself, mama. Now, what can you do with the vision write-up you've crafted? Here are some of my favorite ways to hold on to what you saw.

Read it out loud to yourself. When you read what you wrote out loud to yourself, you're reminding your brain of its importance. It's a double-click to the brain of the vision's significance. You're also making the vision more real to yourself when you speak it out loud.

Place your write-up in a place you'll see daily. If you wrote your vision in a journal, place the journal on your nightstand or someplace you'll see it every day as a reminder of your vision. If you wrote it on a loose piece of paper, hang it on your bathroom mirror, or somewhere else you'll see it frequently.

Make a vision board. Vision boards are placed where you can see them every day and serve not only as inspiration but also as a reminder of what motivates and drives you, and the life you're leaning into.

After you've written down your vision, grab an 8½ by 11 sheet of paper, some magazines, and markers of different colors. Using your vision write-up as your guide, cut out words and pictures from the magazines that align with and remind you of the vision you wrote down. Use the markers to write down words that reflect your vision. I've had clients use a range of paper sizes for their vision board, including a big poster board to capture their vision and place it in their home office, or two poster boards: one for their personal life and the other for their career. Feel free to go all out with glitter, stickers, or whatever excites you, or keep it as simple as possible. You can grab a friend or two and do this as a fun activity together. My two closest friends from college and I did this a few years back in January to kick off our year, and it was full of laughter, fun, and deep conversations about our lives.

Share your vision with someone you're close with and trust. Not everyone has the right to hear your future vision. When you share your vision, read it out loud to your favorite person or people to make the vision further come to life and feel more real. Talking about it in vivid detail is another reminder to your brain that this is really important to you, and it will go to work to remind you just how important it is. Sharing with others can also help keep you accountable to your vision.

Call upon your future self. When you're facing a difficult decision or grappling with something, ask yourself what your future self (who embodies the vision you had) would want you to say and do? What is your future self longing for you to experience, realize, step into, stop avoiding, and decide? What is going to matter the most in one, ten, or twenty years' time?

Pick one aspect of your vision and start working toward it today. What is one step you can take this week to move in the direction of your future vision? And what is one step you can commit to taking the following week, and so forth? Keep the steps small. The culmination of small steps yields massive results over the long term and leads to lasting change.

Just as Nina engaged in her twenty-year vision and used her awareness of what would really matter to her then to decide which steps she needed to take, you can do the same. Your time is not "someday" when certain conditions are met. Someday has a way of becoming never. The time to step into the power you've always had and unleash it is now. Let it rip.

All of it.

OUR OPPORTUNITY TO DREAM

For women of color at the intersection of motherhood and high-achieving professional badassery like Nina, visualization may seem too foreign to even try. We were raised to be practical, realistic, and responsible with our future desires. That's right, even our future desires and dreams had inherent limitations. Most of us were hustling to reach what others take for granted: a quality education, college graduation, and a financially stable and secure job with benefits. Yes, we hustled, because that's what our parents did. We were focused on what we needed to do to make good on our parents' sacrifices, and we desperately wanted to make them proud, as well as the rest of our family and community.

Our parents couldn't role model future visioning for us. They didn't have the privilege to think about their lives beyond fulfilling our immediate essential needs, let alone the time or wherewithal to create the mental space for dreaming. They were so focused on us, they didn't have the luxury to dream for themselves like we do.

My mother sacrificed her dream of becoming a doctor because my parents couldn't afford the tuition for college and medical school. At one point, my father was getting his college degree full-time *and* working full-time, and my mother couldn't do the same thing. They had bills and two little kids to worry about.

My parents' choices and daily reality had ZERO to do with a lack of determination or willingness. Have you met immigrant parents? They're the most determined, hard-working, can't-tell-me-nothing humans on earth. But the where-there's-a-will-there's-a-way mentality is simply not always applicable. There is nuance to life; people face real barriers that add ambiguity and complexity to decision-making. Willpower is not enough to push through and get what you want. To believe willpower is all that's needed creates problems, because then we start blaming ourselves for where we can't go or what we can't do.

My parents worked every day and took care of us, kept us safe, made sure we had a quality education, picked us up from afterschool, and there is not one day I'm not so grateful for what they provided us. For them, there was no room for dreaming, only for surviving. My parents gave me the privilege of the opportunity to dream a life for myself and it was a privilege neither they nor my ancestors could have imagined. My great-grandparents raised my father and his sister (my fabulous Tía Yady) on a beautiful farm in the mountains with a river running through it, in a tiny town in the Dominican Republic. I'm pretty sure the idea of college, let alone law school, never even entered her mind.

To take advantage of this opportunity, we must get out of our own way. We're not in survival mode anymore, but we act like we are.

We aren't our parents; we don't have the same challenges they did. We have more opportunities, which is literally the point of what our parents did for us. We honor

> We aren't our parents.

them and their sacrifices when we own what they've given us and double down on our big dreams in ways they couldn't.

We have to be open to envision what we haven't yet seen or experienced. We're not necessarily going to find evidence of what is possible by looking to the past or to the people around us. Often, a mentor, senior colleague, or leader takes you under their wing, and they're open and honest about what it takes to excel. At the same time, it can be difficult to learn a new way of thinking and navigating the world than you did before, when the feeling of not having enough, belonging enough, being worthy enough, or being good enough dominated your mind.

Here's the thing. I want you to sit in your greatness and power today, starting right now. So, if you've avoided Asking yourself what your life looks like in one, ten, or twenty years, now is the time to get down to business.

ALIGN: Putting It All Together

*"All things are possible! The key is to identify
what you want, claim it for yourself,
and believe that you are worthy to have it."*

—Iyanla Vanzant

C an we please clap it up that you've reached this chapter?
You've done a lot of work, and it's entirely appropriate
and necessary to celebrate yourself in this moment. In
the Align step of the framework, we're going to add deeper layers
to the work you've already done. We'll walk through how to Align
your future vision, the current season of your life, your purpose,
values, strengths, and what gives you meaning with how you're
living each day. You'll see it all come together into a fuller picture.
So, stay with me.

Let's start by reviewing what you've learned and done so far.

- You've learned how to start to let go of self-judgment to take
  honest stock of where you are and what season of life you're in.

- You dug deeper to gain clarity on your sense of purpose, core values, and strengths.

- You opened your mind to envision a future for yourself, be it a one-, ten-, or twenty-year future (or all), and you've committed to taking a few steps to get closer to that vision.

- You've also engaged in deep discernment and introspection, something that most high-achieving professional women of color and mothers rarely give themselves the time, energy, and grace to do. You have. It's a big deal. Take it all in.

BABY STEPS

My goal is to give you a clearer sense of what's necessary to obtain Alignment in this season. Make the decision now that you can do this and are committed to it. Make the decision now that you have the power to live the life you choose, one that is Aligned with who you are, and your vision for yourself.

You'll continue to be an agent of your own change. You'll gain clarity on the decisions and actions needed to bridge the gap between how you're navigating your daily life and what gives you meaning and fulfillment. Combined with what you have Activated (your sense of purpose, your values, and your strengths), the questions you have Asked of yourself (your vision) will serve as your North Star+. These critical, driving elements will remind you of what you care most about in life and why, so you can match your daily actions to them, and live more in Alignment with them.

Sometimes, changing daily actions is not about making massive changes. More often than not, it's about experimenting with small changes to see how they feel and how they work in your life. Consistent and incremental changes are less jarring and threatening to your system. Plus, small changes help to clarify what's truly important and what sacrifices you're ready, willing, and able to make. Experimentation can help prime your brain for bigger changes down the road.

Camila Gets Creative

This was the case for my client Camila. When we first met, she said she was ready to leave her corporate job, a position she worked toward her entire life. But her job for the past two years was not Aligned with what she really wanted to be doing. She was a high performer, but the job didn't allow her to exercise her creativity, which is both one of her top strengths and core values. For Camila, creativity was inseparable from who she was as a person. To feel like herself and alive, she wanted to be challenged with more opportunities to grow and contribute in her unique way. Camila wanted to lead new initiatives or be a part of new projects, where she could be part of the design and development stage, and where she felt she could contribute the most. She was tired of the long hours and sacrificing evening time with her daughter, especially when it was work that she found boring and unfulfilling, regardless of how good she was at it.

Camila reached the point where she was considering looking for a new job. As we delved deeper into her desire to leave, Camila had two critical realizations. The first was about her daughter. Her daughter's school was expensive, and Camila's income was needed. Without her income, her family could only afford to maintain the status quo for six months, if she couldn't find a new job. Sending her daughter to a different school was a sacrifice she and her husband were not ready or willing to make, and dipping into their savings was not an option, either. Thus, Camila would have a tight timeline to find a new job that paid her the necessary salary, and she knew she'd be hustling to make that happen.

Camila's second realization was that she wasn't powerless in her current role to ask for work that aligned more with what she most wanted to do. She could ask to expand her current role and take on a new initiative; she could also do some due diligence about other possible roles at her company that would allow her to flex her creative muscles. Camila started reaching out to colleagues. Whether they met in person over coffee or virtually over Zoom, those conversations gave Camila information about her options. She often said those conversations gave her life; they made her feel like it was possible to be more creative in a role at the company, rather than needing to look elsewhere. She knew that securing that role would take time (because headcount doesn't just appear in different departments), but if she wanted to do it, she knew it was possible.

One year later, Camila is still at the same company, and she's in a different role leading one new strategic initiative with a cross-functional team and serving on another team charged with another highly visible project for the company. She's knee-deep in strategy, design, and development, which is what she wanted more of in her previous role. And she isn't sacrificing as much time with her daughter as she used to. She learned how to create and tweak a new schedule so that it worked for her, and set boundaries little by little, with flexibility for urgent matters, that has resulted in her being less anxious, and more productive with her energy and time. She even took up a creative writing class once a week and took three days off to attend a creative writing intensive so she could further explore that part of her, separate and apart from her day job.

Like Camila, Aligning what's inside of you with what you do each day and how you do it, does not always require a massive or sudden shift. Alignment involves experimenting with different scenarios on how getting what you want would play out in your current season of life. It involves gathering more data to gain more clarity to make an informed decision on the next right step. And it often requires tradeoffs, but not in a this-or-that or all-or-nothing kind of way. Life is more nuanced than that. When I say tradeoffs, I mean amplifying the *most important* parts of your life, which doesn't mean the other parts are not important or should be neglected. I'm not suggesting completely sacrificing one thing for another, rather, choosing *definitely this* and *some of that*. And sometimes one is in service of the other, so we need to allow for that overlap, too.

If Camila's daughter was in public school, Camila and her family would have had more financial options. That's just math. She could've quit her job and worked hard for six months to find the job that would meet her requirements. She could've also decided not to explore any options, stay in her current job, and make peace with her situation. There were many routes Camila could've taken. But in her current season of life, Camila wasn't willing to accept the status quo. She took action to understand her options and decided she wasn't going to settle. She put her energy into learning more about her options within the company and to see if that would work out and it did, even if it took a year. The key is to be honest with yourself about tradeoffs, what you're willing and able to do to explore possibilities, what you choose to prioritize, and why.

"EVERYTHING" IS NOT A PRIORITY

Camila made some hard decisions, thoughtfully and intentionally, about what to prioritize. Prioritization is an effective tool to make life easier. Yes, it makes your life easier. (I didn't say it's necessarily a natural inclination or that it's easy to do!) Overachieving professional women of color ascribe importance to everything, and then we try to do every single thing at a high standard of excellence.

Since a young age, we were taught we had to work twice as hard as others, and to expect the utmost from ourselves. We often cannot afford to make the same mistakes as others. Our mistakes are magnified when we're one of the few. We cannot hide or fly under the radar. The world experiences us as women of color, and so do the people in our workplaces. They see you physically first. And they confuse you with the other Latina, Asian, or Black colleague(s) first. They do not confuse White people for other White people.

But we often grin and bear it. Rarely, do we speak up, because again, we have very little runway when we do speak up. The consequences are greater for us. The consequence is more visibility for reasons other than our work. We were conditioned to ensure our work was so impeccable, it would speak for itself. So, we almost ensured our own success. After all, if you earn straight As and execute with excellence at work, your success can become undeniable.

If we speak up about anything other than our work, it takes the attention away from the work and puts it onto us as people, even when we excel at our jobs. Most of the time, we decide it's not worth the headache, so we often stay silent. We talk to each other about it, but not to anyone else. We don't want to be perceived as "complaining" or "too sensitive" or "angry."

Our standards of excellence and the value placed on hard, exemplary work are the result of the conditioning we've received since childhood. And as we entered school and our professions, that conditioning was reinforced. We did well; we got opportunities, and we kept pushing ourselves in accordance with our high standards. As we continue along in our careers, and have our children, volunteer our time in the community, and take on a host of other responsibilities, we apply the same high standard to all of those things. But the more responsibilities you take on, and the more energy you expect of yourself at the same intensity level, the more depleted you become.

I'm right there with you. This is exactly what contributed to my burnout several years ago. I felt the need to be everything and do everything, no matter the cost to my well-being.

How do you decide what to prioritize when everything seems so important? Everything may feel important; however, there are certain things, people, and experiences that are *more important* than others. Deciding what and who is the *most* important is what prioritizing is all about. Prioritizing doesn't mean the other things are suddenly *unimportant*. It simply means you put a stake in the ground when deciding that spending time with your kids before bedtime is *more* important than catching up on work emails or cleaning the kitchen. And if it's not, no judgment. This is an example only.

Prioritizing means you decide against accepting a promotion—even though you deserve it. You decide against it because you've observed and done your due diligence on the expectations of that expanded role and concluded that taking the promotion means sacrificing critical time with your kids, and they're at a stage where you believe they need you around more and you want to be there with them. You're making a decision (again, as an example) based on this current season and the truths about your situation, including your work environment, that quality time with your kids in the evenings and weekends is more important than taking on added responsibilities at work.

Remember, this is about your current season of life. In two years, you could be in a different season and feel more ready and capable of taking on additional work responsibilities in a new role. We're focusing on what is true for you *now*. And what's true for you now may change in the future.

I'm not saying you cannot have both an accelerating career and quality time with your children. I'm saying you must be crystal clear that those are your priorities in this season, and other things will fall away. They become the decision-making matrix and filter for decisions, like if you're also considering taking on a volunteer role or scheduling mentee coffee catchups. It means those other experiences may have to temporarily take a backseat.

The good news is you've already done the work to understand what's most important to you. From previous chapters, you know what season of life you're in, what you're focusing on, and where you envision yourself going. That knowledge, combined with the core values, strengths, and purpose you've identified in Chapter

7, can drive decision-making and behavior, and they provide useful guidance to make decisions and determine your priorities.

Prioritization 101

With your season of life, North Star (strengths, values, purpose), and your vision in mind, let's do an exercise to decide what your true priorities are for the next six months. Look at your core values and your one-year vision. We're using the one-year vision because, remember, we're setting priorities for the next six months, not longer than that. (If you didn't opt to that one-year vision, you can either do it now or use the other vision exercise you did for this exercise so you don't lose momentum.)

Anchored in your core values and one-year vision, write down your priorities for the next six months. This means you'll list the most important things, people, tasks, and experiences you want to devote your focus and attention toward. Be specific. For example, listing "family, work, and health" isn't specific. What are you doing with family, what's going on with work, and what are you doing to take care of your health? If you benefit from having a structure when creating lists (like me!), use the Wheel of Life categories in Chapter 6 to organize your thoughts on your priorities. I recommend not listing more than three per category. If you list more than three, the next part of the exercise will be more difficult. Here are some examples of priorities for each category:

- Personal well-being
  - Exercise four times a week
  - Thirty minutes of alone time each day

- Therapy once a week
- Journal on Sundays

- Family
  - Quality time with the kids most evenings without checking my phone or laptop
  - Go on a date with my partner (or friend or sibling) every other week
  - Call my parents and sister once a week and put it in my calendar so I don't forget!

- Work
  - Perform job with excellence
  - Don't overdo it or ask for more projects
  - Prepare fifteen minutes before each meeting
  - Go to one professional or extracurricular event per month

- Friendships
  - Take a walk with a friend once a week
  - Go out to dinner or lunch with a close friend twice a month
  - Plan one friends-only weekend every quarter

Do you see the difference between simply saying family is a priority and providing details on what that looks like to you at this time in your life? Because you got specific, you can visualize these activities; detail brings them to life inside your mind.

Before you finish your list, I'm going to take a firm and loving stance on one priority that must be at the top because it's so critical to living a joyful life. That priority must be your mental, emotional, and physical well-being.

You cannot pour from an empty cup. No one shows up as their best for their children, work, partner, or others, if they have not poured into themselves first. I know that's what you want and why you're

> You cannot pour from an empty cup.

reading this book: to understand yourself better, where you need to focus your energy, and what needs to change (or to finally make a change) so you can access more fulfillment and alignment—not only for your sanity, but so you can flourish in this season in your professional and personal life.

Make practicing deep self-care a priority. Deep self-care is all about tending to yourself and creating that space and ability to check-in with and nurture yourself. You tend to everyone and everything else—your kids and family, the cleaning, organizing, your email, what clients, colleagues, your manager, senior leaders, or partners want and need from you, and the list goes on. At the drop of a hat, you often push yourself to fulfill those needs. What about your needs, though? What about how you're *really* feeling? Make *you* the number one, fundamental priority. Without you, the whole ship sinks.

Commit to yourself right now and make one of your priorities YOU. That means carving your time and space for *you*. It means journaling so you can clear mental and emotional space and have some type of output. We are inundated with so many inputs, requests, to-dos, and information all day. Use journaling as an output to write down and get curious about how you're feeling, what you need, and how you can give that to yourself. Making yourself a priority and practicing self-care means saying no to a meeting that can be pushed to next week if you've already made an appointment with yourself. Going for a walk to clear your mind or taking fifteen minutes to relax before the afternoon's onslaught of meetings will pay off dividends over time.

Once you complete your list of priorities, circle the top three that are the most important. I understand all the items are important. However, in this season, you're learning to be laser focused on what's most important. And that, my friend, cannot be everything or you'll stay stuck in uncertainty and overwhelm.

For each of your top three priorities, one of which is *yourself*, write down why these priorities are so important to you. For example,

- Family: Spending quality time with my children at dinner and bedtime is important because I want to continue to know my children as they grow and be able to connect with them daily.

- Relationships: Going on a date with my partner (or friend, or sibling) every other week is important because I want to maintain our connection and have an uninterrupted conversation.

- Well-being: Taking time to exercise four times a week helps me to feel strong, restored, and energetic.

The final step in this exercise is to decide what actions you'll take, including what needs to be shifted, to Align your priorities with what you're doing each day. Prioritization allows you to make Aligned decisions and take Aligned actions. The specific actions can look like the list of examples I provided earlier—i.e., take a walk with a friend once a week falls under the relationships/ friendships bucket. Or, actions can be much, much bigger.

My client Mia was constantly tired in the mornings. No wonder, she only averaged five hours of sleep a night. She decided to prioritize "sleep" so she could have more energy throughout the day. Her goal was to get eight hours per night. Four weeks later, Mia reached that goal, and a few weeks later, even pushed it to nine hours! She did it by eating dinner no later than 7 p.m. and shutting down her laptop by 9 p.m. Instead of watching TV, she got into the habit of taking a shower and reading a page or two of a book (a printed book, not a Kindle or on an iPad) in bed before quickly falling asleep. She landed on that routine by experimenting different nighttime rituals until she found one that made her eight-hours-of-sleep priority a reality.

When you identify your top three priorities, you're committing to the changes that living those priorities will require of you. For closer Alignment between your priorities and your everyday life, there must be *some* change. Even a seemingly small change, or a culmination of small changes over time, can create a huge impact, as they did for Camila and Mia.

Your top three priorities can be used as a filter when making decisions whether to say yes or no to something, be it a work event or any other time commitment. For example, if one of your priorities is to be home for the kids' bedtime, but you have three evening work events in a three-week period, perhaps you go to the *most* important event. Decide what gives you more bang for your buck. Think quality not quantity. This allows you to spend some time with your colleagues, clients, or potential clients, but also stay aligned to your priorities. It requires you to shift from a binary type of mindset to a "less-of-this, more-of-that" mindset. Again, it's not all-or-nothing.

THE PRIORITIES PRISM

Having clarity around your priorities can also help you assess job opportunities, decide whether to leave or stay in your current job, or go for a promotion or new role at work. Many of the women I coach create their own decision-making matrix to assess each job opportunity against their top three priorities. Those priorities tend to fall into one or more of the following buckets: flexibility and work-life harmony, salary and benefits, seniority level, opportunities to grow and make an impact, work environment, pace, alignment with the organization's mission, and the substance of the work (or actually liking the work they're responsible for).

Flexibility is a priority many women share. We discuss what flexibility looks like and why it's important, and it often relates to being able to decide how we manage our time and energy to tend to all of our commitments and responsibilities. We want quality time for ourselves and relationships that are most important to us, our work, our kids, and to maintain our sanity of course. For some, flexibility means remote or hybrid work. How many days will be spent in the office or at home? Is a full-time, on-site position a deal-breaker? For some women, it is, and for others, it isn't. We all have different circumstances, opportunities, and resources; so, one person's professional priorities will look very different from another's.

Regarding the actual work, some women may not like what they do, but they love who they do it with, they're incredibly skilled at it, and they love the financial stability it provides. For other women, if they don't like the work, no amount of money will convince them to stay. There are hundreds, if not thousands, of variations on the different questions related to assessing or seeking professional opportunities including your must-haves or your nice-to-haves. You're only responsible for asking yourself the right questions about what matters the most to you and answering honestly. There are no wrong answers here. There's only the answer that fits with who you are and what you want from your life. Go inward instead of outward for your answers. While mentors are incredibly helpful, external advice only gets you so far. You'll have to make decisions for yourself, which requires that you know yourself and the truths that underlie all of the elements you're considering.

You might experience an inner tug-of-war, and that's okay. Sometimes, what you *need* to do right now is not what you *want* to be doing. Conflicting needs and desires are part of the human experience. Your work is to do your best to resolve those critical conflicts as best you can in this season, based on what you know to be true about you and your life. You resolve them by accepting that truth, deciding what you're going to prioritize, and following through on the decisions and choices that Align with that. If you get stuck, anchor into your vision from the previous chapter. *What do you believe will matter most in one, ten, or twenty years? What would your future self advise you to do?* Use that to inform what actions you need to take today to be more in Alignment with the life you envision in the future.

Recall Liliana, who didn't love her job but waited to make a career move, because her job paid well and one of her top priorities was buying a home for her family. One of the main obstacles we face when we're in a difficult spot is that we resist the reality of the situation. Liliana recognized she was over her job, but she knew it served a purpose: buying a house. This meant she was able to make more peace with the situation because it was in service of what she wanted, even if she had to wait two years to get it. She made the choice to be intentional and stay focused on her priorities, instead of sitting in misery, and you can, too.

THE FEAR FACTOR

Change of any kind—large, small, or even none at all—can feel disruptive, like you're settling, or you're standing still. But change of any kind is significant, and the weight of that significance can bring up all kinds of feelings. You may start to question and doubt your ability to make change happen. You may convince yourself now is not the right time for a change, or you're not ready. You may think you don't want to deal with any change right now because you're still trying to get by. You might think you need some other condition to be met before you can put any change in motion. Pay attention to your discomfort and identify if your decisions are anchored in real necessity or if they're rooted in something else.

I say this with deep love and respect, but sometimes we can be very creative with our excuses, and excuses tend to be rooted in fear. If you find yourself swirling in all the reasons you cannot do or try something different to find joy and alignment, ask yourself: *What am I so afraid of? What am I really worried about?*

For many people, the fear of judgment, rejection, uncertainty, discomfort, and/or disappointing others can stop them from taking the very action that will bring them closer to what they most want and need in this season of life. Not you. You're going to learn how to take action, despite the uncertainty, discomfort, and fear that change can bring. For me, learning about the neurological inner workings helped me to take action so I could live in Alignment with my vision. It helped me to understand what beliefs I was attached to and what excuses I was making.

Fear is rooted in the brain's need to know the outcome, because your brain doesn't like the unexpected and isn't inclined to make change easy. When you're considering making a change in your life, big or small, your brain is going to make it harder than you'd like. You experience the feeling of fear because the amygdala part of your brain, which is responsible for emotional processing and regulation, senses a threat to how things are. When the amygdala detects a threat, the gloves come off. It will activate your body's response system, including the release of the stress hormones cortisol and adrenaline. Those stress hormones prepare your body to fight or flee, increasing your alertness and physiological readiness to handle the detected danger. Your heart rate and breath quicken. Your body needs this kick in the booty to get moving. If there is real physical danger, you need to get the hell out of there.

Thousands of years ago, prehistoric humans needed to be prepared to run for their lives. In modern times, we still need our brains to be alert to danger in certain environments, like when you're walking to your car by yourself in a parking garage. We want our amygdala to sense a threat and activate our bodies' release of cortisol and adrenaline so we can run, fight, or do whatever is necessary to stay safe.

But it's not helpful to have the fight-or-flight stress response when you're considering making a change in your life that doesn't put you in physical danger. Because change is unfamiliar, your amygdala will do its rapid scan-for-threats thing, and scan for danger. The brain does not like uncertainty or the discomfort it creates. Research shows our brains prefer familiarity and predictability, which makes change straight up threatening. Your body will start generating a stress response as if it's in danger when it's not.

So, if you freak out over the thought of change, this is why. It's not your fault. It's how our brains and bodies kept us safe thousands of years ago. The prefrontal cortex, or the logical part of the brain, is almost nonfunctional when your amygdala is fired up and it impacts the decisions you make in the moment. It's very difficult to think your way through emotional responses in real time. Pausing by bringing awareness to your breath for thirty seconds is much more effective to turn the prefrontal cortex back on and get it optimally functioning again.

We need to retrain our brains to understand that change isn't dangerous, and that we'll be safe. Our brains have neural pathways based on repeated experiences and behaviors. Those pathways become ingrained and comfortable, making it easier for us to repeat familiar actions or thoughts. Introducing change requires forming new neural pathways so when your brain experiences a certain trigger, it knows to go down the new neural pathway that produces a different response than the old one. The more you can move through the unfamiliar and unexpected, the more your brain understands that not all situations of unpredictability and uncertainty warrant triggering a stress response.

Another reason the brain doesn't like change is because it's hard work. We've made it easier for our brains by forming habits and automating much of our behavior, like brushing our teeth, putting our seatbelts on, and using a turn signal when you're driving (please tell me you use your seatbelt and turn signal). Without automation, our brains would be working overtime to make conscious decisions every second of the day for basic repetitive tasks. But habit formation helps conserve mental energy and allows us to function efficiently. When an automatic behavior or habit is disrupted by change, our brains expend significant cognitive effort to understand it and scan it for threats. And even when our brains aren't activating our bodies' stress response, they're working hard to make the change stick. There is a catch, though. The brain will attempt to revert to old patterns because they're predictable and familiar. Creating change is mentally taxing (literally), which is why the brain resists it and we feel uncomfortable.

This is why implementing small changes over time is so effective. You're telling your brain, "Everything is okay! Nothing to fear here!" You're priming your brain to slowly learn that positive changes aren't physical threats, and it can relax. Your amygdala can take a beat, and your prefrontal cortex can do its thing.

When the brain's emotional response to fear takes over, it has a hard time functioning. This is why carving out time for the type of exploration and introspection you're doing right now is so important. This is your safe space to give your prefrontal cortex the best chance to process and plan how to move through the fears you may be experiencing. So, when your brain starts to freak out, it also remembers (thank you hippocampus for memory retrieval) that it's played out this scenario before, it's not threatening, and there's no need to fully trigger your body's stress response.

The most common fears I hear about from the women I work with are

- Overthinking = The fear of making the "right" decision because what if all the worst-case scenarios happen?

- Timing = The fear of making a change at the wrong time, assuming a later time will always be better.

- Judgment = The fear others will judge them for their decisions and actions. The typical: *But what will people think of me?*

- Disappointment = The fear they'll disappoint people they care about: mentors, sponsors, partners, children, friends, and parents, among others, for not doing what others would have wanted them to do. And the fear they'll disappoint themselves by not meeting their own (or others') high expectations or standards, or by not accomplishing the goal or change they seek.

- Rejection = The fear that others will write them off or think they're weak or can't hack it.

- Perfectionism = The fear that the change won't be good enough, or that it will cause them to sacrifice their high standards in another area of life that matters to them.

- Failure = The fear that it won't work, and it will be all for nothing. This includes the fear of failing to support one's family or failing in the eyes of others (which is related to the fear of judgment and rejection).

These specific fears are variations of the same overarching fear that things will not turn out the way you want and expect them to. You want a guarantee that the effort you put in will be worth it, that others will still like you, and that you won't lose anything. As we've learned, our brains don't like uncertainty and unpredictability, so of course you want a guarantee! But you don't need science to tell you that life is unpredictable and there are no guarantees. We cannot predict or know what's going to happen in the next five minutes, let alone what the outcome will be if you take action toward your goals.

Because you can't predict the future, your brain starts making up stories to fill in the gap, which are usually the worst-case scenarios, or excuses about bad timing. Yet, your only answer for when a "good" time might be is when some future condition is met: when you get your bonus, when the project or case you're working on slows down, or when things aren't so hectic. But you and I both know that condition won't be met to your satisfaction, or enough to trigger the change you say you'll finally make. So, you'll be in a holding pattern. And you end up doing nothing to get unstuck and live the life you say you want to live. Time passes, and you stay right where you are, feeling the way you feel.

> Doing nothing is a decision. It's not a passive decision; it's a proactive one.

You may not be conscious of it, but doing nothing is a decision. It's not a passive decision; it's a proactive one. Make no mistake about it. You're peppering your brain with all the reasons a change or action cannot or will not work. You're so consumed with internal chatter about the potential costs of making the change that you can't see another perspective, one that can free you from the mental paralysis that fear generates.

And what if I told you that there is a deeper layer of fear, the deepest one in fact that we rarely talk about because it seems so elusive and contradictory? It's the fear that drives all the others we just talked about. It's what deep down you're really afraid of: You're afraid you'll actually succeed, live the life you want to live, and be who your vision has called you to be. You're probably asking yourself: *Why would I be afraid of that—it sounds great?!* It's because you've always been told what to do to be considered "good" and to reach a goal. This happened in your household, at school, and at work. You can measure how good you are and if you reach your goals with grades, performance reviews, and titles. You're told what you need to do to make it to the next level and you commit to doing those things, because it's what you were told you have to do.

Until now, you've done what you've been told to reach this point in your career and life. Whether it's someone who told you directly or messages from society, culture, family, or community that were explicit or implicit, you've been following the rules. You've been following the norms. You've been adhering to expectations. Now, you're daring to do something that would look like a detour to someone else ("Why on earth would you . . . ?"), but it's exactly what *you* want. It's the direction your future self is telling you to go in. And no one knows that future self but you.

Because when you go against expectations, rules, and norms, and you truly start paving your own path, you start scaring yourself. Who I am without these expectations? Who am I without all these sources of validation, with no one telling me if this is the right thing to do? Who am I without knowing what people think of me? Who am I without being directed? You're now the director and that's scary as all hell. That's what you're afraid of.

You're afraid of what it will mean to finally be in the m'f'ing driver's seat. You're afraid of what it will mean when you claim what you really want, and you have to say goodbye to certain things and people in your life who won't ever understand it (and it's not your job to make them understand it). You're afraid you'll lose what you've known. And what you'll gain is almost unfathomable to your mind right now.

As Marianne Williamson aptly describes in *A Return to Love*: "Our deepest fear is not that we are inadequate, it is that we are powerful beyond measure. It is our light, not our darkness that most frightens us." And it's that light and your true power lying dormant right now that you're terrified of. Because what if it all works out, and it's even better than you could have imagined? If you feel every single word you're reading right now, good. It means you know it's true and you know what to do next.

You can still love the mantra bracelets and social media posts that encourage us to be fearless and go for it (showing a picture of Beyoncé, Wonder Woman, and other strong, powerful women). These are inspiring images and encouraging words, but I've yet to meet anyone who doesn't feel fear when they try to do things differently or embark on something new that they care deeply about—all the different layers of fear. For every career pivot I've experienced, fear has always been part of the equation. We cannot eliminate our fear; it's part of who we are.

Babies Don't Drive

Honestly, if fear is not part of the equation, I'd say whatever you're working to change doesn't mean that much to you! But rather than letting fear block us from something new, it can be managed so it doesn't control your decisions. We don't want to let fear sit in the driver's seat of your car. There is no way you're going to allow that. You've worked too hard and been through too much to give up control of what you're doing, where you're going, and how you're going to get there.

So, if we can't get rid of our fear but she wants to drive your car, what do we do with her? We put her in the backseat, like a young child in a booster. You wouldn't put your child in the driver's seat or leave her at home alone. No. You bring her along for the ride and accept what may come in the car. Having her there may feel stressful because you can't predict her behavior. She might cry or screech if she's not happy or something is bothering her like the fact that she dropped her pacifier or something she was holding on to. She may ask for a snack even if she just ate. She might seek attention by kicking the seat or whining. But, she might sit quietly, too. She might be entertained by you singing Beyoncé's *Renaissance* or *Cowboy Carter* albums. My three-year-old is not supportive of my singing. She says: "Mami, no, no, no" when Beyoncé is on (and even the *Encanto* soundtrack), because she wants to hear the singers, not me. Maybe your little one (unlike mine) wants to sing along with you to all the old-school Gloria Estefan and Janet Jackson songs you're playing. She might talk to herself (my personal favorite). For better or worse, your child is your little companion and you accept this reality, which is why you continue to drive with her in the car. The same is true if you take the train or bus everywhere. There is no other option.

Treat fear like she's your toddler. Put her in the backseat and deal with the fact that she may make some noise and be disruptive. Hell, give her a name, Veronica, and talk to her when she wants attention. Maybe you're thinking of asking for a role in a different group (or a change to your current role), a raise, or a promotion. Maybe you're considering leaving a job that feels really comfortable (especially financially) to you, or you're considering saying no to partnership or other type of promotion. There goes Veronica stomping her feet, wanting your attention. She's throwing a tantrum because what if they say no to a raise, promotion, or role change? What if you've now annoyed them and they stop liking you? What if they think you're an ungrateful brat for asking (they may not say it, but that's what they're thinking)? What if they think you're not as good as you think you are? What if they think you're not a team player and you're greedy? What if they say something to hurt your feelings and illuminates and unearths your deepest insecurities? It's better not to know, right? Wrong.

Tell Veronica you understand why she's upset. This is very scary and unpredictable, but you've worked so hard to be able to ask these questions. You deserve answers to them. Remind her she is going to be okay and thank her for trying to keep you safe. You appreciate her concern. You love that she's your ride or die. And you will do this together. You're going to get on the road and place her in her snug booster seat, and you're going to get in the car and drive where you need to go.

Veronica hasn't been neglected or avoided. You've engaged with her. You've given her the attention she needs so she can understand you get her. You get where she's coming from, and you're going to be okay nonetheless.

I've asked every woman I've coached what would happen if their worst-case scenario came true, and they all say the same exact thing. "I will figure it out and it will be okay." See. You forget how resourceful and resilient you are, my friend. You forget your own power to do the very thing you're scared of doing—the very thing that you think will be too disruptive to even try.

So, let me ask you a few critical questions. First, what's the potential cost of doing nothing? What's the potential cost of not making the change that is Aligned with your truth and your priorities in this season? How will you feel if you maintain the status quo? How will things be different if you aren't willing to do something different?

And critically, what if it all works out? What if the best-case scenario happens, or pretty damn close to it? How will that feel? Will you feel better?

You're going to teach your brain to sit in the unfamiliar by actioning small changes, one at a time. Taking steps to create small changes aren't as jarring for your brain. They give your brain time to adjust and to redirect neural pathways and form new habits and routines.

Think about all you've accomplished to this point. I'm sure it was challenging, and you had to remind yourself why you wanted to achieve what you wanted, especially when it got difficult. But the goal mattered to you. Its importance was significant enough that every time you started to question how it would all turn out, you stopped your mind from spiraling, refocused, and got back on track toward your goal.

The change you're seeking now merits even more focus and attention because it's about how you feel about your life and how work fits into that. You deserve to feel like you're not fighting against yourself each day. You deserve to feel like you're taking the actions that are Aligned with your truth and what's most important. You deserve to feel great about your life in this season. Mothering and career don't have to be a constant uphill battle. You can make it easier for yourself. But you have to be willing to look in the mirror and face yourself and your truths. Be willing to face your fears to move into action to fully express who you are and live your priorities to step closer to that future vision of your life.

You have more agency than you give yourself credit for. It means you can change your mind (like today) and make better decisions moving forward (like tomorrow). It means you can work through the fear and discomfort that come with change to take action and Align your behaviors with what you envision on the road ahead. Don't let Veronica drive your car. She doesn't even have a license, and you've got the insurance policy.

PART 3

FIND JOY

Unlearning Old Beliefs

"The hardest thing about unlearning
is letting go of what you thought you knew."
—Alex Elle

Stepping into your power can be tricky, especially if you're holding on to old beliefs that aren't serving you and are constraining you in some way. The inclination to maintain the status quo may be the result of subconsciously holding on to beliefs you picked up in childhood or in the early stages of your career. It can be challenging to feel empowered when you're battling those beliefs. That's why we're going to tackle them right now.

Rising up to claim your truth and living in alignment with it requires understanding how our unconscious beliefs have shaped the way we show up for ourselves, at work and at home. One of the reasons we feel like we're in a never-ending battle in our minds is because of the beliefs we've been socialized to adopt since we were children. We touched on a few of these beliefs in Chapter 2: The Weight of Expectations, and we'll dive deeper into them here.

As we work to dismantle them, think about how these beliefs are showing up in your life and how they may be preventing you from uncovering and owning the truest you and rising up to meet her when it counts the most.

1. BELIEF: RESPECT AUTHORITY AND KEEP QUIET

Growing up and into our careers, many women of color were socialized to be obedient and compliant. I'm not only talking about most households; schools treated us similarly. I went to a Catholic school until eighth grade and I'll say it: I was scared of some of those nuns. I learned to speak only when spoken to. We were taught to be quiet and not make a fuss. It was made clear that if we spoke up, we'd often be bothering someone. We didn't want the stress of causing someone else's stress, so we learned to say less. We suppressed our feelings and opinions to keep the peace.

We were taught to not challenge authority figures and to do what we were told. Respecting authority—the matriarch, patriarch, the teacher, and older relatives—is different from staying quiet and not asking for what you need or want.

Many of us grew up in homes where the parenting style was not democratic; our parents didn't allow for input. We did what they told us to do, and we knew not to question it too much. Often, our parents' parenting style was born out of fear: fear for our safety, fear we would make mistakes or poor decisions, fear we would do something to cause them worry, stress, or emotional pain. I'm the first to raise my hand and say the less-democratic style of parenting helped keep me safe and out of trouble at a young age. I understand my parents so much more now that I'm a mother. Because if I'm truly honest, there are times I prefer my kids to just be quiet. Yes, there, I said it. Sometimes I want them to be quiet and do what I say, and not ask questions or challenge me. Long ago, I accepted my parents did the best they knew how to do. We cannot expect our parents to have the tools to parent differently than they were parented, but we can decide to take all the lessons we've learned and try it another way with our children. We can keep what worked and adjust the rest to parent the way we want; I'm sure our parents tried to do the same.

But for us, being taught to keep quiet and respect authority as a child can manifest as an adult by not sharing your perspective in a meeting or not challenging a senior colleague or leader at work. Your programming impacts you in the moments when you might have a different perspective on a decision or believe something could be done better. You want to say something, but you hesitate. The voices in your head contradict and battle each other: one tells you to say nothing, and the other tells you to speak your mind.

The voice telling you not to say anything runs through all the worst-case scenarios. It tells you the following:

- You're only going to prolong the conversation and there are other agenda topics that need to be covered.

- People don't think you're that smart.

- You probably haven't been paying attention to the discussion. You missed something and if you say something, your inability to pay attention will be on full display.

- Whatever you say is not going to make a difference, so why bother?

These thoughts tend to spiral and feel more powerful than the voice that tells you to speak up, the voice that says you're smart and capable; you're in this meeting to contribute, and you'll feel better about the decision or conversation if you say what's on your mind. If you lean into the comfort and familiarity of how you've been trained to respond, you'll stay quiet and not interrupt the conversation until you proactively retrain your brain and body to respond differently.

The other people around the table may have more experience than you, or be more senior to you, but you've been invited to the meeting for a reason. Let's look at the evidence: If no one wanted to hear from you, you wouldn't have been hired, you wouldn't be on the team, and you wouldn't be in the meeting, period. Stop talking yourself out of your value at the table. You've made it to the table, now own your seat. You've come prepared to the meeting; you're present and focused. Own the reason you're there. And if you still decide not to share your views in that meeting, it's not the end. You may be more of a processer, and need extra time to gather your thoughts before you share them. You can walk down the hall or hop on a virtual call and share your perspective then. You can always make up for a missed opportunity.

2. BELIEF: BE HUMBLE

You may know I have a podcast called the *Humble Rising* Podcast. When I use the word *Humble* in that phrase, I mean the insatiable hunger to learn and grow, and the understanding that our personal evolution is a never-ending journey. The word *Rising* means rising up to meet our truest selves with courage as we work toward achieving success in our personal and professional lives, in the way we each personally define success. But the word humble is not typically used alongside rising in other contexts. And humility is not a word that typically evokes feelings of empowerment and perpetual growth. It's also not what was meant by the word, when we were told to *be humble*.

Women of color often feel the need to downplay or entirely disregard their achievements and ambitions to avoid attention, which appears to the outside world as modesty and humility. There are many intersecting factors that contribute to this paradoxical situation, such as cultural norms, racism, and sexism. We're constantly navigating between societal expectations and the need to assert ourselves to be respected, valued, and recognized in the workplace.

You've heard the wildly sexist, yet incessantly repeated, feedback women get; they're told they need to be "more confident" and have more "executive presence" to advance in their career. Well, the research shows that women are faulted (and fault themselves) for not advancing in their careers because of their "lack of confidence."[1] The overemphasis of confidence as a career accelerator or doomer for women neglects the other qualities critical to impactful leadership: vulnerability, inclusion, adaptability, demonstrating calm in high-pressure situations, and cultivating a psychologically safe environment. In those situations, we want thoughtful, intentional, and honest leaders. We don't need the guy who makes a hasty decision, who doesn't ask the right questions, but who conducts the meeting and renders a decision with "confidence" and "clear communication." In those situations, everyone loses: the leader, the team, the company, and the stakeholders.

But the message instilled in us to be humble is connected to the message to stay quiet. We were told: work hard. Keep your head down. Don't cause trouble. Stay in your lane, and success will come. And then do it on repeat. Intellectually, we all know that working hard, keeping our heads down, and keeping our contributions and achievements quiet is not the formula for accelerating in our careers. Yet, we hold back in the moments that matter for advancing ourselves like asking for a promotion, an expanded or different role, or a specific case or an opportunity. And then the opportunity passes by. We say, maybe next time. And unless you equip yourself with strategies to be more at peace with the discomfort that comes with asking for what you deserve, the same thing will keep happening.

We have to practice making the big asks and having the uncomfortable conversations. We have to practice talking about our achievements. So, the "next time" you prepare for your end-of-year performance review at work, list everything you've accomplished, especially the things that may not be immediately visible. If your company doesn't ask for a written self-assessment, reach out to the decision-makers to share what you've contributed. If you win an industry award or receive recognition from your alma mater, tell your manager at work. I'm not advocating for walking around the office telling every single person or blasting out emails about all your wins. I'm talking about informing the people who should know about your awards and achievements—the ones that stand out as a culmination of your hard work, determination, and commitment. I was never good at this I have to admit, and that's part of the reason I'm sharing it with you now. Learn from what I could've done better.

Recognize your wins and allow others to celebrate them with you by tactfully sharing them. You don't lack humility when you share noteworthy recognition; you're allowing others to share in your joy. And if you struggle with truly feeling the abundance and joy that comes with recognition for a job well done, you have to give yourself some time to honor it. Each time, you have to pause to pat yourself on the back, because you earned it. When we don't let ourselves experience joy and when we don't let people share in our joy, we miss opportunities to connect with ourselves and others. We miss opportunities to allow others to be there for us.

3. BELIEF: BE GRATEFUL

The belief that we must always be grateful runs parallel to the belief that we need to be "humble." Both are deeply ingrained, and both serve to keep us small, to prevent us from asking for more. They reinforce the notion that our situation is "just the way it is," and we should be grateful for what we have and stay quiet.

Here's how it shows up in our adult lives. You get a job offer! Yay, be grateful! Instead of negotiating a higher salary with additional benefits for the job you're perfectly qualified for and have earned, our ingrained gratitude tells us, "Hey, you should be grateful you got the job offer at all. Don't push for more. Be grateful."

And when you see a salary amount you've never seen in an offer before, you're inclined to take it without asking for more, especially if you didn't grow up seeing that kind of money. So, you don't negotiate. And when, a few years later, you're struggling to find your place at work, or you're clear about your role but feel stagnant and aren't sure what's next, you don't tell anyone. You don't ask for a new challenge or learning opportunity. When you see others getting promoted or working on highly visible matters or projects, you stay quiet, even though you want access to those same opportunities. This could also apply if you're looking to exit your job or exploring the possibility of leaving. The belief of "just be grateful" sucks you right back into settling because again, *why do you want more anyway? Be quiet and be grateful.*

Part of the resistance to asking for more or exploring it is because you don't want to be a bother. You don't want to be perceived as greedy, the squeaky wheel, or ungrateful for every opportunity you've had thus far. See how this works? Gratitude is important when it comes to taking stock of our lives and appreciating our many blessings and gifts, but it can also be a mental trap.

When you don't ask for more, you're allowing others to believe you're happy right where you are with what you have. And if you undervalue what you've delivered and bring to the table, no one is going to place a higher value on it. There are enough systemic barriers and challenges in the way at work, which we only scratched the surface of in Chapter 3. So, it's imperative our minds don't become yet another obstacle to asking for what we deserve.

Years ago, when I received a promotion, I was on maternity leave and didn't think to negotiate the new salary, which was a minimal increase. I didn't realize it then, but I was so grateful for the promotion I didn't even think to negotiate for a higher salary. The person who shared the news with me was the leader of our group and a mentor of mine, so I could have easily asked, but I didn't. Fast forward to a year later I started talking to people at my level about what they made. The conversations happened organically because we were friends and worked closely on projects together. I found out I was making less than my colleagues who had a similar scope in responsibility and remit. So, I went to work. I sat down and typed up all of my contributions over the past year and my current high-impact projects to provide evidence of why I deserved a higher salary. I also added the exact salary I wanted, to be crystal clear about what I was asking for and why.

I scheduled a meeting with my boss/mentor. Writing out the evidence to make my case for a salary increase was one thing. Having the conversation was another. As the meeting approached, I started to feel uneasy. Remember, this person was someone I deeply respected and admired, who had worked with me for years. He had given me numerous professional opportunities, time and time again, and now I was about to ask him for *more*. But I knew I deserved the increase, and I decided the worst thing he could say was no. I went to the meeting prepared. He looked at my contributions and the higher salary request and responded, "Of course, we can take a look at this. You didn't have to write a memo on it!"

All that worrying, and he was immediately open to exploring it. He said he'd get back to me soon, and he did. Shortly thereafter, I not only got what I asked for, I got much more—nearly twice the increase I asked for. That wouldn't have happened had I not asked. And despite the initial trepidation I felt, I was happy I'd decided to ask for more. I'm not saying you'll get what you ask for every time; rather, it's about not letting the belief that *you should be grateful for what you have* prevent you from asking for what you want and deserve.

Trying to convince yourself to "just be grateful" for what you have can also block you from asking for and moving toward what you most want and need in your life. We've all been there. You're feeling stagnate or stuck in some way, and you're longing for more, but you talk yourself out of doing anything about it. We often use gratitude to convince ourselves it's better to stay where we are than to explore what "more" could look like. We weaponize gratitude against ourselves as a means to stuff down how we really feel and what we're experiencing instead of acknowledging that gratitude can exist alongside desiring more for yourself and your life. It's in recognizing this that we finally learn to give ourselves permission to move toward what we're longing to have more of.

4. BELIEF: SUCCESS IS DEFINED BY TRADITIONAL MARKERS OF SUCCESS

Regardless of whether they were spoken or unspoken, we picked up messages that success means owning a home, obtaining a college and/or graduate school degree, securing a financially stable job, getting married, and having children. This is especially true if you grew up with immigrant parents or in a home where money was scarce or financial insecurity. Success, in some circles, may mean owning a Mercedes instead of a Honda. It may mean having a fancy watch or a vacation home or designer clothing. Some people love and can afford to buy a Mercedes—i.e., they're not over-leveraged or carrying significant credit card debt. And if you love Mercedes (or anything else) and have the financial abundance to buy it, I'm all for that! Do you, boo. Live and love your life. Enjoy it.

But too often, the reason we buy and do things is not for pure enjoyment or our love for it. It's because of what having or doing those things means to us and what they signal to others, especially our communities and families. They're status symbols of our success according to societal and cultural norms and expectations.

When I was a young attorney, a senior attorney told me all the partners had luxury cars because clients would think less of them if they drove anything else. At the time, I drove a 2001 silver Toyota Corolla with manual windows and locks. I went to check out the car with my father and bought it outright for $4,000, cash. It was the first car I got with the money I made working at a law firm between my first and second year of law school. The car may not have been anything special to others, but it was special to me because I earned it. My father helped me keep it in mint condition, so much so, that I eventually gave it to my sister and then my uncle. That 2001 Corolla became a family heirloom.

When we long for things (like a car), we must ask ourselves why we want them. I needed a car because I didn't want to take a bus to school in the early mornings and late at night. The reason I bought the car was practical. Buying a car to impress someone, or to show off your "success," is not. In fairness, sometimes when I buy shoes, it's not practical at all. It's because I love the color hot pink. I don't need new hot pink shoes, but I enjoy the way they make me feel. But I've also bought clothes and jewelry to conform to a certain image of success, such as a pearl necklace and earrings as a junior attorney, even though I didn't like them. Other women attorneys wore them. I thought a successful attorney was supposed to wear pearls, so I did, too.

Beyond the material things, your job title itself is a marker of success. Ask yourself: *Why do I do what I do? Do I like the job, or do I like how prestigious it is and how it makes me look to others?* The first time I truly thought about this question was when I decided that becoming a partner at a law firm was not for me. I knew if I stayed and went for partnership, I'd be doing it for the wrong reasons: to prove to myself and others that I really was smart and capable, and to show the Latinx community that we could make partner with less than 2 percent Latina law firm partners. I didn't love those reasons because they were about what partnership symbolized to others, while I would be the one sacrificing my time and energy to achieve it, including time with my infant son. It was not the life I wanted.

When I left the law firm, I went to work with a former colleague in a legal and compliance department at a growing biotech in a lower position than I had at my firm. It was not a lateral move; it was more like a step back, and I took a huge pay cut. But it felt like the right decision because I was Aligning how I felt with what I was doing. I believed I was meant for more and I was exploring what that "more" could be. A title was not going to bring me happiness and fulfillment. Titles may bring more money and credibility in professional circles, but how I defined success and the meaning I ascribed to it had changed. My definition of success was a lot different when I was twenty-five than it was when I was thirty. And it's changed again now that I'm in my forties. My priorities have shifted throughout the different seasons of life, and I'm more than okay with that.

How do YOU define success in this season of your life? Is it rooted in your three-pointed North Star (values, strengths, purpose) and future-self vision?

5. BELIEF: STRONG WOMEN DON'T ASK FOR HELP

I grew up in a family of strong women. From my great-grandmother to my aunts, the women in my family loved hard, worked hard, and have endured hardships I can only imagine. They experienced stress and emotional pain, and they never complained. They didn't talk about their emotions at all. They stepped up to every challenge and pushed through, and they supported each other. But that support was often reserved for family only because personal business was not to be shared outside of the family. Even my sharing my experiences growing up in this book is a major risk. We're expected to keep personal business private and not to share too much about our lives, especially not on social media or in a book like this. But I believe owning our truth is about honoring our stories, which includes talking about people who've deeply impacted us like our families.

Here again, what an incredible lesson to learn as a child: You have the strength and grit to navigate any challenge, and if asked, your family will be there for you. While we picked up the importance of strength, resilience, and family, we also grew up believing we always had to be strong in front of others. We were not to show weakness to anyone outside of the family. Weakness signaled we were vulnerable and could be taken advantage of.

If there was a problem, you weren't going to dwell on it. There was no such thing as sitting in your feelings because "What's the point of that?" We didn't wallow in the past, either, because "What good would that do? We can't change the past." You learned to figure out how to move through whatever challenge you faced and handle it. You sucked it up and pushed through. You were always moving. *Siempre pa'lante* (always forward).

One of my favorite lines from my twenties was, "I'm a Vargas. We get shit done." While it rings true, it's also why I struggled for so long to admit when I needed external support with what would become my anxiety and depression. My anxiety and depression knocked me to the ground for months. I resisted accepting this truth, and finally when my cognitive functioning declined and my panic attacks became more regular, I knew I needed help. I didn't even tell my parents what was going on until I was on medical leave. I knew they would be supportive, but I didn't want them to worry, and I didn't really want to discuss what had brought me to that point. I was exhausted. The thought of sharing what I was going through was equally exhausting. When I finally did share, I wished I had told them sooner. They got it. They saw me for me and were a huge part of my support system that helped me get better. I underestimated them precisely because of an internalized belief that I had to push through, and that's what they'd expect, too. I was wrong.

Although my parents understood, a diagnosis of anxiety and depression is still perceived as a personal weakness in communities of color. When you consider what our ancestors and the generations before us went through, this perception makes sense. Racism, sexism, and colonialism have caused our communities deep suffering and have shaped our experiences and narratives. There are also stereotypes and microaggressions perpetuating the idea that women of color are supposed to be strong, independent, and capable of handling everything on their own. We feel social pressure to conform to these expectations and resist asking for help. We feel like we can't let our guards down, much less ask for support, which only reinforces our need to be strong and self-reliant.

Although you may have internalized the message that you need to always be strong, and appear to have it together, that pressure can lead to neglecting your personal well-being and emotional needs. Unlearning this belief starts with recognizing and bringing awareness to it. Every change starts with awareness.

So when you think about the limiting belief that strong women don't ask for help, has this belief manifested in your own life? If so, how? How does it impact your friendships, relationships, and work life? How can you give yourself the support you need? Who can you ask for your support and when will you do it (give yourself a date/time or reach out right now)?

6. BELIEF: SACRIFICE IS THE NORM

Similar to the belief that you always have to be strong and self-reliant, many of us grew up learning that life is all about sacrifice. We saw our parents work hard for every single penny they earned. We didn't ask for certain material things or experiences because we knew they could neither afford them nor take the time off from work to buy or do them. Many of our parents fought to keep us on the right track in school. We experienced their exhaustion, frustration, and stress. We saw them mistreated because of their race and ethnicity. They prepared us for a world they knew wouldn't always be kind to us because of our racial and ethnic backgrounds. And they would do anything for us, especially sacrifice their own desires and needs. They rarely did things just for themselves. I don't recall my parents ever going on a date or on a vacation without my sister and me. Ever. I don't recall them ever doing anything just for themselves. We knew their hard work, blood, sweat, and tears were all for us. It was how they expressed their deep and profound love for us.

Because we grew up witnessing our parents' constant sacrifice, it's natural for us to believe self-sacrifice is always required, and that it's the norm. This belief manifests in our adult thoughts and actions in several ways.

- You strive to achieve a certain level of financial and professional success according to societal standards and expectations to make good on your parents' sacrifices and to give back to them.

- You shame yourself for feeling overwhelmed when things get difficult.

- You tell yourself your parents had it harder; they sacrificed everything for you, so you shouldn't complain.

- You think anything worth having requires constant sacrifice and striving for; it isn't supposed to feel good.

- You can't enjoy your life because you're always on to the next task, just like your parents were. They never stopped and neither do you.

This is part of the reason we feel like we're running on a tread-mill set at a high incline. Let me tell you this. If your parents could have eased up on the sacrifices they had to make, they would have. If your parents could have spent more time with each other without their kids, they would have. Just like you, they were once parents of toddlers, and they too felt like they were going to lose their minds. You don't think they would have wanted a break, no matter how much they loved you? Of course, they did. They're human.

We often forget that we aren't in the same survival mode as our parents. We have more choices than they did. We can choose which sacrifices we want and need to make and why. We may not like the choices we have, but they're choices, nonetheless. For example, you might sacrifice doing work you love to make money and support your family. You might sacrifice dinner with your kids because you have to work late on an urgent matter. You might have worked your ass off for years, logging sixty-hour-plus weeks, and had to sacrifice other parts of your life.

Sacrifices are a part of life, but they cannot be your entire life. It cannot be the common theme in every season. That's not your story; it's your parents' story experienced by you as a child. But you're not a child anymore. You can create the life you want in ways they could not. Now is the time to take advantage of the opportunity they gave you to do that.

7. BELIEF: REST IS LAZY AND UNPRODUCTIVE

You may have grown up in a family that prioritized productivity, performance, and selflessness over rest and self-care. My parents were always on the move: working, going to school, taking care of the house, raising their children, and helping their brothers and sisters. I rarely saw them rest. There was always something that needed to be done and family to spend time with. My parents couldn't afford to outsource household responsibilities, so my father learned how to do projects himself like finish the upstairs of our house (twice) and fix cars like a pro. He learned by reading manuals and books. There was no internet back then. He essentially became a carpenter and contractor on his own. If his final product wasn't perfect, he worked on it until it was. He didn't leave things unfinished and worked every weekend on a project, almost nonstop. My father is retired now, but to this day, he's always working on something and loves learning how things work.

Let me be clear, there is immense value in being instilled with the belief that you should be mindful of your time and how you spend it. There is a difference, however, between believing you must use all your time wisely and believing you must be "productive" with all your time. Because of our upbringing, as well as racist stereotypes and assumptions we're trying to overcome, women of color often feel guilty when we aren't doing enough. We have to be constantly doing something that signals productivity and commitment—be it working, serving on boards, volunteering, cooking, cleaning, organizing, or anything else.

The need to be productive is a belief that results in doing things beyond what's necessary to manage our daily responsibilities. We make ourselves do things that aren't necessary or aligned with what's most important and where we should be focusing our energy. We say yes when we mean no. We organize for the third time even when it can wait. We don't even realize we're doing things to feel like we're on the move, because that's what our bodies and brains are used to. And then we wonder why we can't rest. We literally feel restless when we get still, because it feels so foreign to us. On top of that, when we're constantly switching between work and home modes, we can feel guilty for working and tending to our responsibilities as parents and vice versa. We can feel like we aren't doing enough.

At work, the intersectional challenges cause us to feel like we have to constantly prove ourselves, work harder, and show we're capable and deserve to be in the spaces we occupy. We work tirelessly to overcome the systemic barriers that are in the way of advancing our careers. This manifests by placing the needs of colleagues or managers above our own. When we get the nonurgent email at 10 p.m., we respond. We say we respond because we want to be responsive, but it's not about responsiveness. Responding the next morning is also responsive. Unless we are, for example, at trial or in the middle of corporate deal closing, the email isn't urgent, and we know it. This is about being seen as the one who can be counted on. This is about wanting to be liked. We're so focused on not wanting to disappoint people that we sacrifice health and sleep to stay up late to email them back. We don't get the rest necessary for cognitive functioning and physical, emotional, and mental well-being. Think of it this way: Is responding to emails when you should be resting and sleeping worth your health?

Rest and sleep are non-negotiable. A study in the *American Journal of Epidemiology* found that adequate rest and sleep play a significant role in maintaining hormonal balance. As we know, hormonal fluctuations can cause changes in our mood and energy levels and impact our overall health. Studies show that women who get sufficient sleep have a reduced risk of developing chronic conditions such as heart disease, obesity, and diabetes.[2]

The belief that rest is unproductive impacts way more than your professional life. As a mother, you tend to prioritize our children's needs over our own. And when you're not working or taking care of your family, you still see so many other things that need to be done—e.g., birthday party planning, preparing for guests to visit, pictures that need to be framed, drawers of your kids' clothes that need to be organized, putting away toys and crafts for the second time today because the mess drives you mad, or removing the bright purple marker drawing on the wall that magically appeared when only your two-year-old was in the room.

Yes, there is a lot that needs to get done. I'm with you. I can always find something "to do." Just because I can find something that needs my attention and I have a list of to-dos, doesn't mean they all need to get done at the same time. You and I both know there will be more things to do tomorrow. There's always stuff that needs to get done. This is why it's critical to carve out time to re-energize and give your mind and body a break consistently. Rest is not a luxury; it's fundamental to your well-being.

8. BELIEF: I'M NOT GIVING BACK ENOUGH

How many times have you heard the phrase "to whom much is given, much is required"? Luke 12:48 of the Bible, states, "From everyone who has been given much, much will be demanded; and from the one who has been entrusted with much, much more will be asked."

As you can imagine, I found a plethora of theologian interpretations when I was researching this phrase. Colloquially, it's often misinterpreted to mean that because you were "given" opportunities and support to reach the position you're in, you have the obligation to give to others in a similar way. Of course, people have supported you and helped open doors for you. But none of what you have achieved came out of thin air. You worked hard to be visible and considered for opportunities. Mentors, sponsors, and employers don't give opportunities unless you've demonstrated you've got the goods.

And, my friend, you have the whole package. You have unique talents and gifts. You've acquired a set of skills and expertise, and you've worked your ass off. This was true before you had kids and it's true now, too. Kids consume a substantial amount of mental, emotional, and physical energy and time. The time you used to have to give has largely been replaced with the time it takes to care for your children and spend quality time with them. You're giving back to the next generation who need your guidance, support, and unconditional love.

Women of color often bear the emotional labor of fighting for social, racial, and economic justice and helping their organizations with diversity, equity, and inclusion (DEI) efforts, whether it's serving on a committee, or spearheading initiatives focused on DEI. But this can lead to burnout and exhaustion, especially when none of these efforts are typically rewarded come performance review time. What's more, studies also show the expectation to always be the strong one, the resilient one, and the selfless one contributes to women of color feeling invisible when it comes to doing this work. It can undermine our sense of well-being.

Saying "no" to someone you want to support feels like you're not only letting that person down, but also possibly letting down members of your community. You want to say yes because you want to help. You want to be the person who says "yes" because you feel you should be able to handle everything on your plate and give back, right? You think more is expected of you because of your level of success and what you represent to your community. In this way, you may also feel you're letting yourself down.

Giving back takes energy and time. If you have children, you had more time to dedicate to the causes and organizations you were passionate about before they came along. You could chair a gala event, sit on several boards, chair committees, and volunteer to be on every career panel for professionals of color. I've probably sat on more than fifty career-type panels over the course of my career and moderated my fair share of panels, too. I've had more coffee chats with upcoming professionals of color, especially lawyers, than I can count. And here's the thing. I love meeting and staying connected with them. It took me some time as a budding lawyer to find a community of lawyers of color that I could vibe with and who provided me with honest advice. I've had mentors and sponsors of color (and White men) who have gone to bat for me when I wasn't in the room and who have been instrumental in providing me with advancement opportunities. But the responsibility of paying it forward and giving back to a community that has given to us can weigh heavily.

It's a burden and a blessing to be in this position. On the one hand, it's a blessing to have achieved a certain level of career success and be in the privileged position to share your perspective, time, and energy with others. Despite the challenges you've faced, you've gotten where you are through hard work, persever-ance, betting on yourself, and grit. On the other hand, the weight of expectations to be the trailblazer; the mentor; the advisor; the representative of all things; the diversity, equity, and inclusion (DEI) expert (DEI is assumed to be your area of expertise sim-ply because you're a person of color); and to always be available to give back to others can be a heavy burden to carry.

DECIDING TO UNLEARN

Unlearning deep-seated childhood beliefs and shedding cultural expectations is a complex and ongoing process. This isn't a box you check off, or a one-and-done exercise. The experiences and beliefs of women of color are diverse, and everyone's pathway toward gaining clarity and finding joy will be different.

Shedding is the result of Asking what your future holds, and the shedding is necessary. It typically happens, when people are already years into their careers versus when they're in high school or college. But I have discovered through my coaching work, the decision to start unlearning can be sudden. It can happen in an instant, when one day, you say, "Enough." You say, "I'm done." And you start to unpack all the old thinking patterns and beliefs and relearn a new way—a new way that allows you to show up fully as yourself. And that journey is never-ending, but I can tell you that even embarking on it is so freeing. I invite you to get curious and raise your awareness, which is the start of changing how these beliefs impact your everyday decisions and actions.

For instance, explore the following scenarios and experiment with challenging yourself to respond differently than you have in the past. Ask yourself questions that start with "what" and "how" to prompt your brain to provide a specific answer. Dig beneath your brain's first response. Then, be honest with your responses.

You're in a work meeting and you hesitate to speak up.
Ask yourself: What is the reason I'm staying quiet in this meeting?

You've been in your same position for a few years, and you've been contributing at a high level and adding tremendous value over time.
Ask yourself: What is holding me back from asking for a promotion or a raise?

You're struggling to ask for help at work or at home.
Ask yourself: What is holding me back from asking for help?

You're staying in a job you don't like, that's unfulfilling, or you're not getting what you deserve and want in your role or at your workplace.
Ask yourself: What is the real reason I stay? Do I love that reason?

You're told it's time to decide whether you'd like to be considered for partner and stay on the partnership track.
Ask yourself: What do I feel when I think of partnership—i.e., does partnership excite me, make me curious, or bring me a sense of dread?

If it's the salary, what number do you need to hit each month? Can another job fulfill that need? See if you can pinpoint the root of what you're doing and the reasons behind it. This will help raise your consciousness and awareness, so you're able to see it happening in real time and show up more intentionally in that moment. It will also help you make more intentional decisions about your life instead of defaulting to the old, familiar, ingrained belief system that has held you back. Sometimes unlearning beliefs simply means bringing more awareness to them, and then we can slowly and intentionally begin to dismantle or rebuild them to better suit the life we want to create.

THE HEALING PROCESS

In her memoir, *Finding Me*, Viola Davis describes living in poverty as a young girl in a rat-infested apartment with barely any clothes to wear or food to eat. As an adult, Viola's acting career generates more than enough money to buy a spacious home. In her book, she recounts a conversation with her mother in her new, pristine kitchen. Viola reveals, for the first time, that she and her sisters were sexually molested by their brother when they were young. Her mother has no response. Viola observes, "Success pales in comparison to healing."

Unlike success, unlearning old beliefs and healing isn't shiny. You don't get credit for it and there is no external, immediately noticeable award or recognition. You don't get paid more and there are no bonuses for the most healed. That's part of why healing is so important; it's only about what's inside of you and the experiences and feelings you need to process and move through to live a more Aligned, joyful life.

If you're tired of always battling with yourself and the

negative mental chatter that takes up way too much energy and space, healing is going to give you more peace than traditional markers of success ever will. And if you're chasing another person's or society's definition of success to be happy, you're going to be chasing it for a very long time. Sometimes, you reach a goal you've been working toward, but you don't feel the way you thought you'd feel. Because there will always be another title to strive for or box to check. Each box leaves you with a feeling of accomplishment, but it's fleeting. There's an emptiness you can't explain.

Happiness is not a destination, and it is not a box you check off. Let's shift how we view happiness. It's more like a fluid emotional state that can take many forms throughout your life. You can always get *happier*. This is why I have not used the word "happiness" much throughout this book; I've used phrases like

> Happiness is not a destination, and it is not a box you check off.

owning your truth and feeling joy and fulfillment, which is also not a destination. It's an ongoing journey of Assessing, Asking, Activating, and Aligning your values, strengths, sense of purpose, and vision with how you're living and working in this current season. Instead of chasing, we need to focus more on inner alignment and healing.

All the ingrained beliefs may be part of what needs healing within you. I won't know, only you will. I do know that if you don't heal the relationship with yourself first, you'll interpret what's said about or to you as a personal deficiency. You'll continue to take things personally. You'll allow conversations, feedback, and events to define you and continue to dictate your feelings and experiences. This is one area where you can take the reins now.

Maybe your feelings of unworthiness and never feeling good enough finally need a deeper dive. You'll have to stop lying to yourself and stop trying to convince yourself that how you feel is no big deal, that you're over it. Because you aren't over it, and suppressing your feelings is not going to make them disappear. Avoiding your feelings by working more or drinking isn't going to make them go away. Moving to a different city or country won't do it, either. You simply cannot run away from yourself. Wherever you go, there you are. (Thank you, Confucius.) And your thoughts, feelings, behaviors, and patterns will be there, too. You have to be willing to face the parts of your life that you've been terrified to look at honestly.

Healing is the most powerful enabler of personal agency. It allows you to address past traumas, societal, familial, and cultural pressures, and straight up pain. It enables you to lay a more solid foundation for a strong sense of self-worth, a foundation that isn't dependent on producing and performing at a high level or seeking validation and affirmation from others. If you're constantly relying on external approval, there's a decent chance you're living the life you think is expected of you rather than the one you want for yourself. Remember, your worth is innate. It exists because you exist. You

> If you're constantly relying on external approval, there's a decent chance you're living the life you think is expected of you rather than the one you want for yourself.

don't have to prove yourself or work to earn your worth. It simply cannot be earned, and that's the entire point.

One technique I've used to heal old wounds is to engage with my inner child, my seven-year-old self. I know she's trying to protect me when she tells me I'm not enough or that I shouldn't take the leap when I'm afraid to. When I was a young lawyer and told myself I was going to be harder on myself than anyone else, that was my seven-year-old self trying to protect me. She didn't want anyone to hurt me. When I used to be quiet in meetings, that was her trying to protect me so I would not feel bad about making a fuss. I tell my inner child, "We don't need to say yes to authority simply to please them or to avoid being perceived as challenging. We can say no. And we can make our own decisions based on what feels right to us."

You can practice this, too. Tell your inner child that you can be who you want to be. You don't need the approval of others to feel loved anymore. Tell her you're committed to not disappointing yourself. Tell her it's okay to be afraid to make a decision that might disappoint someone and thank her for protecting you all those years. Hold her hand and tell her, "It's okay, we'll get through it together." I learned this technique from a brilliant healing energy practitioner when I was deep in my own personal suffering. Her help came at the exact time I was ready to receive it.

For me and the many women I've worked with, deep healing allows for more openness to feel inner acceptance and peace. When we look at ourselves and dig deeper than we have before into our experiences from childhood through today, we learn to face ourselves honestly. We confront the truth at the root of the negative emotions and self-talk.

Deep healing allows you to see how your busyness is a coping mechanism. "I'm so busy" or "I'm just tired" or "I don't have time to think about these things" gives you an excuse for not having to confront the truth of your life, who you are, who you're becoming, and where you're headed. I'd like to gently invite you to ask yourself

- Are you the person you want to be?
- Are you the mother you want to be?
- Are you the leader you want to be?
- Who do you want to become?
- Do you feel *good* about yourself and your life?

Healing leads to honest answers to these questions and gives you an opportunity to rise up to a more meaningful, joyful, and fulfilling life. Healing allows you to move away from unhealthy coping mechanisms like working to exhaustion, the glass of wine you always drink to unwind, or distracting yourself with your phone. To be present in your life, you must be present with yourself first.

Healing is personal. You'll have different needs, experiences, and methods of healing. Your healing process may change according to your resources, home or work environment, and support system. It isn't for me to dictate your healing or the way you engage with it. I've experimented with channeling, healing energy, guided meditation, therapy, and more. And there are wounds I'm still working on healing. Healing is a process for all of us. As long as we're engaging in the process honestly, we'll see progress. We'll see the changes in how we speak to ourselves as well as how we interact with those we love and work with.

Healing, like happiness, isn't a goal to be achieved. There's no finish line. There's no end product. I know; it's incredibly satisfying to reach a goal and say you did it. I'd love to shout from the top of a mountain, "I'm fully healed! No more work to do here!" Unless I've reached enlightenment, that isn't going to happen. Instead of thinking of healing as a finish line, goal, or finished product, consider recognizing it as a process of creating more peace within you. You'll notice small milestones of progress. You'll see it and feel it within yourself. Maybe you'll reach a point where certain thoughts about your worthiness or fear spiral less. You'll be able to catch yourself and bring more awareness to how you talk to yourself and why and understand the real reasons for your decisions and actions.

When we're open and engage in the healing process, it not only has a positive impact on ourselves, but also has a positive effect on our relationships with our families, friends, and colleagues at work. By addressing your own wounds, you can foster healthier connections, communicate more effectively, and establish and reinforce boundaries that are in integrity with your values. You can have more fulfilling and supportive relationships. As I'll explain further in the next chapter, the longest study on happiness ever conducted found quality relationships are the greatest predictor of living a good life. To feel connection, love, support, and a sense of community for navigating this current season and future ones, relationships are critical. Finding your people and support system as you continue the work along this journey is where we turn next.

11

You're Not Alone

*"Anything is possible when you have
the right people there to support you."*

—Misty Copeland

B eing open to the process of rising up by gaining clarity, finding joy, and Aligning your inner and outer worlds becomes easier with the right support around you. You cannot and should not have to do this alone. And if you look around, you'll be reminded that you're not. There are people in your corner who want to help.

THE SCIENCE OF RELATIONSHIPS

Research has consistently shown that relationships play a critical role in our overall well-being. Strong, healthy relationships with family, friends, and romantic partners are directly associated with greater life satisfaction and happiness. The Grant Study, the longest longitudinal study conducted on happiness led by researchers at Harvard University, found close relationships are the key to living a good life.[1] The study followed participants for over eighty years and discovered those who had strong social connections and meaningful relationships were happier, healthier, and lived longer.[2] While many of the participants were White men, other longitudinal studies have yielded similar findings that quality social connections are the strongest predictors of happiness, among more diverse demographics.[3]

Not only do studies highlight the positive long-term effects of close relationships, they also show positive social interactions release hormones like oxytocin and endorphins, which are known to naturally boost your mood. Maintaining close social relationships also provides a sense of belonging and support, particularly during challenging times.

Without relationships, we lose our connection to others and the meaning and joy those connections provide. Research also shows that loneliness and weak social connections lead to serious consequences. Not only is loneliness associated with reduced work performance, but it shortens life expectancy—so much so that the health risks of loneliness are similar to the health risks of smoking fifteen cigarettes a day.[4] For women, work exacerbates this loneliness crisis. Sixty percent of women in leadership positions say their feelings of loneliness or isolation actually increased as their careers progressed.[5] Women of color report higher rates of loneliness at work than White women.[6]

Knowing how vital close relationships are to our joy and well-being, why do we often neglect them? We claim we're busy with work and with our kids, and it's true: We work tirelessly on both fronts in addition to our other commitments and obligations.

When it comes to our jobs, they take up far too much of our daily existence, and many of us are still living to work, instead of working to live.

Many of us are not tired only due to our number of working hours; we're tired because of the demands on our energy from our multiple responsibilities at work, at home, with family, in our communities, and more. And I'm saying it: you're also tired because of the time you spend on personal devices, social media, and binge-watching TV shows. These are legitimately fun activities when you have the bandwidth and energy to do them, and you're intentional about when and why you're doing them. You want to laugh with some of your favorite Bravo TV? Go have at it. Someone gives a show a glowing recommendation and you're down to watch it? Go for it. You want to look at funny parenting memes for ten minutes because it reminds you we're all winging this thing? Scroll away. That's all intentional. I'm stressed at work so I'm going to distract myself with Instagram and scroll away. There is no reason for the Instagram scroll other than what it's distracting you from. Can you shut it down when you start feeling shitty about yourself from playing the comparison game on social media, or when you realize it's 2 a.m. and you're only on season three of nine of *Suits* on Netflix? (Season four is even better than season three, by the way, so I understand the desire to keep watching.) But shut it down and go to bed, mama.

With everything we're managing, we have little time for ourselves, much less for those we care about and ourselves. We feel incredibly overstretched. How did this happen to us? Many of the answers lie in how we have been socialized and programmed from a young age and when we entered the early stages of our careers. Since childhood, we've been socialized to be independent, self-reliant, and pursue "success" in our careers at the expense of our own well-being and our relationships. This makes sense. When we started our careers, we went all out. We wanted to prove ourselves and felt we had to. We wanted to make a strong first, second, and third impression with those we worked with and for. We worked tirelessly to live up to our own standards of excellence.

We didn't have the obligations we do now, because we were in a different season. We could have a last-minute dinner or lunch with a friend, go on a date night with our spouse or partner, and plan girls' weekends. Another mother will never ask you, "So, did you do anything fun this weekend?" or "Were you able to rest this weekend?" I love Mondays. Because, in this season, weekends can feel more exhausting than weekdays with young ones. Honestly, I find them to be fun and exhausting, running around, trying to keep the kids occupied or entertained. We know it goes downhill when you won't let your child have the popsicle at 8 a.m., but by 4 p.m., you might give them that popsicle whenever they ask for it, just to have some peace.

When you ask other mothers with careers how they manage all their responsibilities, many say they have support. Support is especially vital when you're facing seemingly insurmountable obstacles and challenges, aiming for new goals, and making changes in your life, even if it's one small step at a time.

Support can come in the form of resources and relationships. Resources include financial capital for childcare, tapping into extended family, hiring the occasional babysitter, and taking advantage of after-school programs. Relationships can extend far and wide, from your own parents to the parents of your kids' friends, but in this chapter, we're going to focus on three key supportive relationships:

1. Partner or spouse

2. Community

3. Friends

These three vital relationships have had the most impact on me and the women I've coached, as they've worked to rise up, gain clarity, fulfillment, and get in Alignment in their lives. These three supportive relationships can help you conquer this season of life as well as the transitions, challenges, and ebbs and flows that lie ahead.

YOUR PARTNER

The first person you need to talk to and ask for help is the person you live with, who's going through the grind with you every single day: your partner. For clarity, I'll use the term partner throughout this chapter. Partner could mean your husband, your wife, or significant other. It could be the person with whom you have children. If you're co-parenting, this section still applies due to the support you need from your co-parent. The partner relationship is also the relationship women talk about the least, which is why it's first on this list. Yet, I wrestled with whether to tackle the need for a truly supportive partner in this chapter. Partnership relationships involve a complex and evolving dynamic with multiple dimensions and nuances. It's not my intention to address and solve all the challenges unique to each type of partnership: divorced or separated and co-parenting, married and co-parenting, or living together and co-parenting. There is no one-size-fits-all blueprint or guide for how to have a successful, loving, and lasting marriage, or partnership.

And, if you're one of the 52 percent of women who are single or separated, and desire a partner, this section is worth reading to further refine what you're looking for in someone.[7] And if you chose not to get married, don't ever want to get married, do not want a live-in partner, or a partner at all—do you, boo! You don't need me to tell you this, but you don't need to have a partner or live with someone to feel fulfilled in life. Period. Focusing on you, your motherhood journey, and/or your badass career sounds amazing.

In this section, I'll mainly focus on dual-income households where two partners are living together, married or not. But, hell, I'm no relationship expert. I'm sharing what I've learned from the women I've worked with who tick every relationship status box under the sun.

More than half of Americans talk to their spouse or partner first when they have a personal problem.[8] If you're married or living with your partner, your partner is one of your primary sources of support and one of the most significant relationships in your life.

As I write this, my husband and I are working toward how to manage all our responsibilities at work and home, while staying connected with one another. There were months when our conversations became limited to logistics about taking care of the kids and the house. Due to my husband's eighty-plus-hour work-weeks, I took on far more of the burden in the house and with the kids. I begrudgingly started to accept this was the state of our relationship (at that time), and I found a way to emotionally shut him out so I would no longer need him as my confidant.

Eventually, we came to a crossroad and had to decide whether we wanted to initiate changes and work on really being friends again. Practically, this meant adjusting our schedules, bringing back date nights, going to couples therapy, and going to individual therapy. It also meant I had to start working on letting go of years-old resentment and anger from past situations when I felt neglected, unsupported, and unappreciated. We're both working on taking accountability for our part in the state of our relationship. We've had to have difficult conversations, and we both have had to put in the work, and we're still doing the work.

The specific circumstances and intricacies of my relationship are not going to look like yours. We're all different human beings with different experiences, wants, needs, and expectations. But my conversations with hundreds of women about their relationships when both people work and parent, plus the scientific research, tell me my general experience is not unique.

A Pew Research Center study showed that in 29 percent of marriages, where both spouses earn about the same amount of money, women still spend more time on housework and childcare responsibilities than their husbands. On average, mothers spend 12.2 hours on caregiving each week compared with the 9 hours fathers spend. The study specifically examined caregiving responsibilities in parents with children under eighteen in the home. Regarding housework, mothers do 5.1 hours per week, while fathers do only 2.2 hours. Mothers spend 19.6 hours per week on leisure activities—hanging out with friends, getting their yoga or boot camp workout on, or binge-watching *Insecure*, *The Crown*, or *Suits*—compared to the 23.9 hours fathers spend.[9]

Beyond the division of labor that remains unbalanced in opposite-sex marriages, the lack of quality time and personal space is real. You aren't alone in feeling like there is no time for your own leisure activities. The demands at work and at home raising young children lead to overwhelm and exhaustion. Your personal needs matter, and they need to be fulfilled while tending to your parental responsibilities.

Being able to create space for yourself, while feeling like you're not failing at work and with your children, is especially challenging for women of color. The cultural expectation is that family always comes first. This means your kids come first. You take care of and sacrifice for your children, the way your parents sacrificed for you. The expectation is also that you put your husband first and take care of his needs, including his sexual needs. You cook for him and your kids each night, just like your mother did. She never complained and neither should you. And you're expected to manage all these spheres effortlessly, leaving you to wonder: *What about me and my needs?*

This is why having a supportive partner is critical. We aren't living in the same world our parents or our grandparents did. Although their perspectives are more difficult to change (and that's not our job or within our control to change), ours are still fresh. And we can have partners who share the modern perspective that equity in a partnership while raising children together is a top priority. Just because you're the woman does not mean you need to cook every night of the week, and it doesn't mean it's all on you to take care of the home. These are internalized and antiquated cultural expectations, and we can feel a deep sense of shame—like we are bad mothers, bad partners, or bad wives—when we don't meet them.

Now, if *you enjoy* being primarily responsible for taking care of the home and your kids, and you feel supported by your husband in other areas that are important to you, go with it! I know many women who love cooking every day for their families, and that's a beautiful thing. Some have strong boundaries where they stop working at the same time each day to make dinner for their family. They've done that for years and it's a priority for them. Others tend to receive support from their partners in other aspects of their lives, like being supported in a career change. Or, if they have the resources, they can outsource support, so they don't lose their minds.

We have to remember that previous generations often had support from neighbors, friends, and family. When I was very young, my aunts and my parents' friends took care of me because they all lived close by. My father's grandparents helped raise him, and my mother's aunt helped to raise her. Today, extended and even immediate family can be geographically dispersed, so it's much harder to offer and receive real-time support with meals, childcare, and love. Our parents and grandparents didn't have to keep up with the demands of work the way we do, household duties, children, and the technology that enables 24/7 access to us, which has blurred the lines between work and our personal lives. But we have these challenges, in addition to perhaps having less family and close friends nearby to lean on for support.

Again, there is no one-size-fits-all here. But if you're emotionally, mentally, and physically exhausted, and you're struggling under the weight of expectation to be the exceptional mom, leader, wife, and everything else, it's time to loosen your grip on the expectations you've internalized. It's time to vocalize your needs and express how your partner can best support you. Sometimes your partner supporting you more means you both agree to hire more outside support or your partner picks up more of what's on your plate. We know that mothers of young children in particular spend more time working, caring for their children, and doing household labor than fathers do.[10] And we need to pay attention to the negative emotions, distress, and work-family conflict that are more likely to increase for mothers, as the result of juggling all those demands.[11] Research also shows that a mother's happiness and mental health can be increasingly compromised due to the time demands of parenting and the ability to direct the path of their careers.[12] Thus, there is much at stake.

You'll have to be honest with yourself about the current state of your relationship and the demands on your energy and time, so you can speak up about what you need. I'm inviting you to be honest with yourself and explore where that honesty takes you. However, this is a two-way street. Is your partner willing to discuss the division of labor in the home, openly and honestly, and make adjustments? Are you able to work toward open communication and collaboration together? If not, what is getting in the way? Does your partner support your growth and evolution? Does he or she help you Align outwardly with what you most want and need inwardly?

There are things we need help with that our partners may not be willing or able to provide. We may then need to decide whether they must be the one to fulfill those needs. If your partner is not and cannot provide the support you need, what can you do to make a change within your realm of control?

There are points in every relationship when you must decide what you're willing to accept about the other person and what you're not. If you truly accept them, you learn to let go of the resentment and feel a sense of peace. That's the goal anyway. If you don't accept them or understand their limitations, you'll be constantly engaged in a battle for what you need and want, and peace won't come, my friend. We can't force people to fulfill our needs. We can only express what we need; we cannot control how they respond. I'm working on this too—I'm not immune to anything I'm sharing with you.

So, if there are things your partner is not able to provide but you can make peace with, what does that mean practically for you? What do you need to let go of, and how can you live with more peace? No one can give you these answers, because no one is you living your life. No one is in your relationship but the two of you. And there is no judgment either way; there is only the truth—your truth. Throughout this book, you've been invited to explore your truth, anchor yourself

> Explore your truth, anchor yourself in it, and take action to make it real.

in it, and take action to make it real, and we must do that with our relationships, too. In addition to the support of a true partner, this becomes easier when you have a supportive tribe that supports and understands you.

YOUR COMMUNITY

Connecting with your community can offer a safe place of validation, understanding, and a sense of belonging. Community can take on many forms in different spheres of life, and often reflects shared interests and a support network.

Women and women of color often face unique barriers and biases in the workplace, which can impact our career advancement and work-life integration. Building a supportive community with others in and outside our chosen profession can help us navigate these challenges and find strategies to move through them with more ease. We share tips, information, and resources that can be immensely helpful when integrating parenting and professional responsibilities. We also exchange strategies for finding childcare options, navigating workplace challenges, and accessing career development opportunities. Sometimes, we end up sharing resources like the name of a favorite babysitter, a house cleaner (this was a game changer for me), and even a house organizer who can help put your kids' toys in order and handle the closets.

Finding your people is about tapping into a network of people who get you without having to explain your experience to them or how to say your name correctly. Building a strong network with other women of color or attorneys of color allows you to connect with people who have faced similar obstacles, have overcome them, or are working through them. This networking can lead to valuable mentorship opportunities, advice, and professional growth.

When I was working at a law firm and going to law school, one of the attorneys from the firm later became my boss when I went to work in a company's legal department. He was a sounding board and has supported me through several career pivots. And one of the judges I clerked for always had sound career advice and challenged me by saying, "It's not about whether you'd be good at it. You would. It's about whether you'd like it." When I had a miscarriage at eighteen weeks, she was one of the first people who reached out to me to offer her support. As a mother herself, she knew the depth of what I was going through and stepped up to be there for me.

When I attend conferences and events especially with other women of color professionals and lawyers, I always leave feeling inspired and empowered. There's a special energy in those rooms that stays with you long after the event is over. More than that, those connections are the basis for not only expanding your professional support network, but also for building long-lasting friendships. One of my closest friends is a fellow Latina I met over ten years ago at a Latina lawyer breakfast. Although we've been through many career and life changes, including having children, our friendship wouldn't have been possible without a shared commitment to grow our own network at an event for lawyers.

WHERE YOUR GIRLS AT?

Yes, this subheading is a play on the 1999 song, "Where My Girls At" by 702. Do you remember it? It was the girl anthem before

"Run the World (Girls)" by Beyoncé. Both songs are about the power of connection among women and what we can accomplish together. Like a community of women, deep friendships foster a sense of belonging and understanding.

At least twice a year, my two closest college friends and I go on a *retiro* (retreat) at the beginning and in the middle of each year. One January, we did future visioning for the year ahead, vision board kits and all. On one of our summer trips, we went horseback riding and talked about the substantial changes happening in our lives, including my friend's baby on the way and my book writing journey (you're reading that book right now). We talk about relationships, work, fears, doubts, struggles, and what we really want in the future. We check each other, in a kind and loving way, when one of us is getting stuck in old stories or beliefs that aren't serving us. We know each other so well; we can hold up a mirror for each other. And then, we have a lot of fun and laugh hysterically.

One of my favorite trips was when we recorded an Instagram reel with an ocean water background featuring us lip-syncing to Ariel's "Part of Your World" from *The Little Mermaid* when it came out in 2023. We went under the "water" and popped our heads up when our turn came to sing a line. We are grown-ass women and mothers, lip-syncing to a *Little Mermaid* song, on an Instagram reel with a fake water background. We laughed so hard that I definitely peed myself a little.

Whether we are laughing, crying, recording a reel, or on a walk-and-talk, our time together fills our buckets. It's why we always schedule our next trip within a week of the one we just finished to make sure it's on our calendars. If it's scheduled, it's real, and it will happen. We get excited in anticipation of seeing each other again, on the heels of the sadness we always feel when we have to say goodbye. Those two are my girls, through and through. Who are the women in your life, who have your back and who you can lean on?

When we're doing our best to take care of everything at work and home each day, we often neglect the very relationships that will help us navigate this tug-of-war with more ease. Research shows nearly half of women say their relationships with friends and family have suffered because of work demands. Our desire and drive for self-sufficiency, independence, and professional success—which is not itself a bad thing—can morph into social isolation. Carving out the time and energy to invest in and nurture our connections significantly contributes to more fulfilling and joyful lives. Women of color are less likely to experience work-family conflict, such as decreased job satisfaction, greater levels of stress, and poor mental health, when they receive social support.[13]

Have you ever gotten together with a friend and had a little more pep in your step or felt like you were on an emotional high afterward? Or maybe, you felt calmer and more at ease. Maybe they made you think deeper or differently about something. We need these kinds of connections to make it through the rough periods of our lives, especially the current season that seems to pit work and home against each other in epic battles. We forget how important friendships are to fill up our cup when we need it the most.

Your girls are critical to being open to receiving support, to feeling more energized, alive, and affirmed. It's a form of self-care for sure. For the purpose of this conversation, I'm assuming you know your friends must be an additive to your life. They cannot suck the energy or joy from you, criticize you, or cut you down. You don't have that kind of energy to spare, and you cannot afford to have friends who bring you down. I'm talking about the women who lift you up, who are like your sisters. Focus on those women. Double down on those friendships. They're the ones that will last. Those friends will be by your side when shit gets rough and crazy.

Your friends provide the emotional support you need, and it's a bonus (but not necessary) when they are women of color with intersecting identities as mothers and professionals. Friends allow you to share your experiences, frustrations, and wins, and you receive validation of your struggles and encouragement. My retiro friends are both Latina like me and they understand what it's like to be first-generation in this country, with parents who came from Latin American countries. We understand each other, and when we send memes to each other about Latinx parents, we laugh because we get it. We get each other.

While mentors and more senior professionals are helpful and well intentioned for career advice, our close friends are also good resources in this department. They know who we are on multiple, deep dimensions, not just in our professional lives. One of my closest friends is a financial guru, and for fun in her spare time, she helps colleagues with their personal financial budgets. She got me into learning about real estate and how it can create passive streams of income so you aren't trading your time for money. And I've read several of the books she recommended to get me started. I'm fortunate to be able to tap into her source of wisdom on a wide range of topics.

Recall Tiffany from Chapter 6, who, in her own view, had neglected her personal relationships. She had several close friends she hadn't been able to vacation with in years. She repeatedly made excuses about not having enough time due to work demands. But once she decided to prioritize spending time with her friends, she booked a vacation with three of her closest girlfriends and came back feeling refreshed and reenergized. She told me how much she had missed them and all about the helpful conversations they had about how her life was really going. Being with them reminded her it was necessary to make changes so her work didn't take over her life, especially the relationships that mattered most to her.

Relationships—the lift-you-upper, not the tear-you-downer ones—are imperative to finding joy even when the days are long. They ignite us. They make us feel more alive, and they're a source of support, guidance, and validation necessary to grow, evolve, and experience life with all its challenges, uncertainties, and unknowns.

Take the time, right now, to text two people you adore and tell them how much they mean to you. Maybe it's your mom, your partner, or a friend. This will take not even ten seconds. Tell them how much they mean to you, and that you're looking forward to hanging out. Then, follow through, and make a plan.

Remember, whether it's your partner, a great professional tribe, or a group of girlfriends who have your back, these relationships are worth investing in for the long haul. They're worth doubling down on. Nurture and grow them, and allow them to fill up your cup.

Unleashing Your True Self

"What I know for sure is that you feel real joy in direct
proportion to how connected you are to living your truth."

—Oprah Winfrey

ronnie Ware was an Australian palliative care nurse who cared for her patients during their last days of life on their deathbeds. Based on the profound truths and admissions she heard and observed from them, she wrote a book called *The Top Five Regrets of the Dying*. Do you know what's the number one regret people had about their lives? "I wish I'd had the courage to live a life true to myself, not the life others expected of me." The remaining four regrets were (in order of priority)

- I wish I hadn't worked so hard.
- I wish I'd had the courage to express my feelings.
- I wish I had stayed in touch with my friends.
- I wish I had let myself be happier.

Here is the great news. You're not dead yet! We'll all die at some point, but it's not too late. My father used to always say, "Death is the only guarantee in life." Though I often rolled my eyes and thought his comment was ridiculous, what he said was true. We don't get to decide how we die, but we do get to decide how we live. And being physically alive doesn't mean you feel alive, which is living in alignment with the truest you that you can always tap into to get anchored and centered.

Paying attention to how you feel, what you want and need, taking care of your relationships, those you love, and yourself, and ensuring work is part of life—not the entirety of your life—are all critical to finding joy and Alignment. This is more challenging for us, as professional women of color, who are mothers, as we navigate more complexity, bear the weight of a different set of expectations, and grapple with unlearning the beliefs that don't serve us. You know what they are by now.

- Respect authority and keep the peace.
- Be humble (in the "keep your head down and be quiet" kind of way).
- Be grateful.
- Success is defined by traditional success markers like titles and salary.
- Strong women don't need to ask for help.
- Sacrifice is the norm.
- Rest is lazy and unproductive.

Healing from these beliefs is hard because we grew up with very little, if any, discussion about our feelings, emotions, or past events that may have caused trauma to our own parents. And for ourselves, we continue to run on the treadmill and fall into the same pattern as our parents. We make excuses that we are too busy for healing, and "What's the point in going backward?" When we mistakenly believe that ignoring the past is the only way to move forward, we forget that our past has open wounds that continue to cause suffering today. Those wounds still hurt because they haven't healed. We can continue to ignore them, but they'll continue to hurt until we tend to them, ease the pain, and find some relief.

LIVING YOUR FULL TRUTH

Have you ever stepped back and taken notice of a woman who passes you on the street or walks into a room? Her mere presence is magnetic. That's not simply confidence you're seeing. That is a person living in her full truth, so much that it radiates out of her very being. It's such a rare thing, that when you see it, you're caught by surprise, and you take a moment to pause.

Living in your full truth is the key to rising up, the key to moving from uncertainty and confusion into clarity, confidence, courage, and joy in your career and personal life. Each step of the 4-Part Framework—Assess, Activate, Ask, and Align—requires re-centering and anchoring in your truth. Your truth is your deepest desires and needs. Your truth is who you are when you remove the weight of all the expectations you've internalized

from childhood into adulthood. Your truth tells you never to settle, stay quiet, or stay small. It calls you to respond to the whisper
(or scream) inside that tells you something has got to change,
that this can't be all there is, or that you're meant for more.

Your truth is always there,
waiting for you to shine a light on it.

It's waiting to be lived. It's not something you find out there;
it's inside of you.

As you've learned throughout this book, there is no magic wand
you can wave to instantly be granted clarity on who you truly are,
what you most want and why, and how to have the courage to live
in alignment with that. And no book can go as deep as you need
to help you heal. I wish it could. I'd be the first in line to buy it.
My own healing and the healing of women I've coached has been
through therapy, reflection, healing energy work, introspection,
and a readiness to be honest.

What works for you may not work for someone else. What
makes you feel alive and gives you energy may not be the same
for others. How you choose to navigate the challenges you face
will undoubtedly be different from how someone else does it.
Although how we initiate change in our lives will differ, we all
start moving toward change when we acknowledge the truth of
how we feel about our lives and ourselves.

I started this book with the moment I broke down after
having my son, feeling lost, tired, and completely unhinged. Facing the truth of that time in my life and then moving toward

feeling better, not perfect, was vital to my healing and to feeling good. Over time, I was able to start aligning how I wanted to feel and what I wanted to do with my actions and behaviors. I was anchored in my values and what mattered most to me, what gave me a sense of purpose, and what I needed to make life a bit easier for myself.

And since that moment, almost ten years ago, I've reached several crossroads in my personal and professional life that required me to go through this framework again and again: after my third child was born and I transitioned from the law to leadership development in human resources with an intermediate step of leading employee relations, and when I decided to leave my day job and become an entrepreneur full-time. There were multiple inflection points, but those are the major ones that forced me to Assess my priorities; Activate my purpose, values, and strengths; Ask what I envisioned for my future; and create Alignment between my inner world and my outer one. These are the steps I used to create the 4-Part Framework I've shared with you in this book.

YOUR NEW NORMAL

When we embark on change and maintain that change for a period of time, we reset our baseline. That new baseline becomes our norm. It becomes the way we operate, until something else disturbs it, or we decide that baseline is not conducive to how we want to live anymore. It's natural and human to want to evolve as we get older, have more experiences, and gain more insights. And it's also totally normal for you to want something—like getting married or having a baby (or another one), two of the biggest decisions we can make—and then feel a sense of loss and grief over your previous life, and to occasionally want your independence again.

You're not weird. You're not crazy. This season of life is what can feel crazy. You can feel unhinged and not like yourself. But you're the constant. You're the one who sets the intention for your day, week, month, year, and life.

This is what the women I've had the privilege to work with have learned to do through the 4-Part Framework. It's what I hope the framework does for you. It's a tool to navigate personal or professional crossroads, or a moment in your life where you're out of Alignment. This can mean massive change, small changes over time that culminate in huge results, or no change at all. The point is your decision to change and the magnitude of change you embark on is just that: a conscious, intentional decision. It's not simply the product of the passage of time. You have the capability to do something different than what you've been doing. You have the capability and the tools of the framework to take the reins and decide how you want to live, mother, and work. You're equipped with what you need to start, or to continue your journey to rise up to claim your truth, the joy, and the fulfillment you deserve, which is long overdue.

PERFECTION IS A MYTH

I'm not suggesting life is going to be a breeze, free of stress and challenges and uninterrupted space and time to pour into yourself the way you need. There will be times when you're simply aiming to get through the week and manage your commitments to work and the kids and your philanthropic engagements. That's reality.

I'm a mother of three young children. Do you know how I create space and time for myself? Oftentimes, I leave the house. Being in the same physical space with my children is an invitation for them to interrupt me. I don't blame them for this. They are tiny humans who want to be close to their mama. They want to be with me when I go to the bathroom, take a shower, go to the grocery store, you name it. Moms with teenagers and older children always tell me to cherish this time when my kids want to be around me 24/7, three sixty-five. I respond the same way each time: "The years may seem short to you, but the days are very long for me." Because to me, the days are still long.

And I still struggle with giving my commitments the full attention I believe they deserve. One year, on my kids' first day of school, I was determined to walk them into their classrooms for the occasion. I woke up an hour earlier that morning. We left the house with plenty of time to get to school, on a typical weekday. But not on this day. Traffic reared its ugly head. I anticipated ten minutes of traffic, not twenty-five! As we sat in the car, inching closer and closer to the school, the minutes ticked by. By the time we finally pulled into the entrance, I only had two minutes to get them in the front door, or they'd be marked late.

I had a choice to make. I could turn left, park the car, walk them to their classrooms as planned, and accept that they'd be marked late. Or, I could turn right, drive up to the front door, and have my son walk my daughter to her classroom. I decided it was better for them to be on time, and my son said he was more than happy to walk with his sister. I, meanwhile, felt like a total failure. I thought: *I can't even manage to walk my kids into school on their first day without making them late!* Then, I remembered that dwelling on the morning wouldn't be helpful to me or to them. It wouldn't change anything. And we could try again tomorrow.

The next day, we did things differently, and we weren't in such a rush. We left the house earlier than the day before, I parked the car, and I was able to walk them to their classrooms and spend fifteen to twenty minutes talking to their teachers and the other parents. It felt good, and I felt some amount of redemption.

Things like this happen all the time. We go through these moments of panic, doubt, or just feeling bad about how we're parenting. We feel bad about being stressed around our kids, or we lash out at our partners for not taking the trash out immediately after we asked. We feel bad we don't have it more together. There are times we lose our patience, forget to breathe, and wish we handled certain interactions more calmly and intentionally. This is motherhood. We're not perfect. No one is.

But you know what makes it worse? Beating ourselves up when things don't go the way we planned or expected. This is a challenging season we're in, my friends. It's batshit nuts, sometimes. We make a misstep, and we immediately conclude it must mean we weren't cut out for this mothering and professional thing. But that can't be further from the truth. You were meant to be a mother doing your thing professionally, with all the fire and light you were born with.

BELIEVE WHAT'S POSSIBLE

Your life is happening right now, as you read these words. It's a privilege to decide how we'd like to live our lives, to decide to have the courage to live it in Alignment, to decide that what once worked for us is not going to work anymore, and then to be able to do something about it. We have the freedom to do that.

All you need to do is believe it's possible to live the way you want to live and feel the way you want to feel. If you're open to believing it's possible, then you're open to learning and growing by applying the 4-Part Framework outlined in this book. You'll be able to take steps to get closer to the core of who you are and feel the fulfillment and ease you long for, even in the thick of your current season.

If you're still hesitant, consider this: What's at stake if you continue with the status quo? What's at stake if you continue to say "someday" and place conditions that must be met before your time to rise will come? Your ability to feel great about how you're working, mothering, and living is what's at stake. Your joy is at stake. You're at stake.

You have the choice to keep struggling and suffering (and complaining) or to move closer to joy and fulfillment, even if it requires that you try things you've never tried before and possibly disappoint others' expectations of you. But you cannot disappoint yourself here. You have to live with you. No one else can live your life. And our time here on earth is limited. We don't get to decide when we go. Unlike money, time is nonrenewable. We can't get it back, so we have to be intentional about how we spend the rest of it.

But here's the good news: This is just the beginning for you. If you've been on a personal growth journey before finding the words on these pages, consider this a continuation of it. Our growth and evolution do not end. It's never done. It goes on and on until we pass on. And if this book was your first introduction to increasing self-awareness, gaining clarity, uncovering your own truth, envisioning future possibilities, and Aligning what's inside with what's outside, I'm honored you chose it. And you should be so damn proud of yourself that you did.

For all of you, know this. Not many will take the actions necessary to change how their life has unfolded. Most people will continue in default mode. They'll continue to move from one day to the next without an intention for how they want that day to go, who they want to be in their interactions with others, and how they'll treat themselves. But not you. You're not going to settle. Women like you and me, we know there's more. We know we can live our lives more fully, and we're never settling for "fine." We aren't settling, period.

To embark on making a change, large or small, personal or professional, requires courage, and a lot of it. It's not something that will come with time. We generate courage when we need to. It's a decision, and you can make that decision right now, right here, today.

Choosing change can feel difficult but difficult does not mean impossible. It just means we have to be more laser focused. It means we have to support each other. It means we have to take care of ourselves, because no one is coming to save us. We've been waiting for far too long to be given a break, or to be shown how to be a woman of color, leader, and mother (and all the other things) and how to do it so we feel fulfilled, aligned, and truly alive. There is no blueprint. You're creating your own unique blueprint.

This season of life is your time. You don't need anyone's permission to begin moving closer to your truth and what you need and want. You're more powerful than you could ever know. You have the power to create the life you want and deserve. This is your time to exercise it. This is your time to rise, mama. Go get it.

KEEP THE MOMENTUM GOING

 For additional support on how to go deeper and put this book into practice, go to www.ariveevargas.com or scan the QR code on the left. You'll find additional resources and all the information you need on my coaching programs, courses, and workshops to support you and cheer you on as you move forward in your journey.

Download and subscribe to the *Humble Rising* **podcast,** featuring empowering stories, expert advice, and valuable insights on how to do this thing called life. In-depth conversations delve into everything from healing and unlearning beliefs that hold us back, to actionable strategies on how to create fulfilling lives and careers. Listen to the *Humble Rising* podcast at https://humblerising.libsyn.com. The podcast is also available on all major podcast platforms.

Access all book-related resources at ariveevargas.com.

ACKNOWLEDGMENTS

'll always be grateful to God for putting this book on my heart and placing it in your hands. Every day, I thank God for the gift of this wild, beautiful life and the calling he's asked me to answer while on this earth. God has always been faithful and devoted, even when I couldn't see it. When my own faith has wavered in very dark moments, God found a way to stay close to me and shine the tiniest light for me to give me hope in the unseen. He didn't just show me that light; he made sure I felt it in my bones. There is no doubt that this book was part of God's plan for me, and for you.

There are too many people who have deeply impacted my life and this book to name them all here. I must start, of course, with my parents who laid the foundation for all I am. It's because of you that I have a fire in my belly and a dangerous tenacity. It's because of the perseverance you role modeled that I've been able to summon the courage each time I've pivoted in my life and career, including one of my most vulnerable actions: to write this book. Thank you for all you do for our family and all the unconditional love you show us and *los guellireros* (your *nietos*)! I couldn't do what I do without your support. I love you more than words can express.

To my children, Julian, Maya, and Thali. You are my everything. Thank you for teaching me life lessons in patience, presence, aliveness, joy, and one of the deepest forms of love a human can ever experience. I will always say yes to your laughter and silliness, and to our singing and dance parties. It's my life's greatest honor and privilege to be your mom. I hope this book makes you proud.

To Trevor, your love, encouragement, and steadfast support means the world to me. You gave me the space to write this book in the early mornings during the week and on the weekends, and to take care of myself throughout this process. Thank you for supporting me in bringing this gift to the world.

To my *hermana*, Clari: You have been through the ups and downs of life with me. Thank you for always cheering me on, supporting me, and reminding me of how far I've come. I'm so blessed to have you as my sister. Salt-N-Pepa and Selena forever!

To all of my family, I'm proud to be a reflection of all of your love, tenacity, and fabulousness. To my great-grandmother who passed years ago and my husband's grandmother who passed away in 2023, know that your legacy carries on. I hope I'm able to live a full life of fierce and courageous action with a massive dose of gangsta energy as both of you.

To my girls (you all know who you are), thank you for truly seeing me and for your love and support. Special shout-out to Diana, Carla, Amelia, Leah, Elke, and Vanessa, who not only are part of my ride-or-die tribe and help make the most challenging seasons easier, but also read earlier drafts of this book. Thank you for pushing me to dig deeper, cheering me on, and for always being there for me.

To my mastermind tribe, the dream of entrepreneurship became real when I met all of you. You gave me the gift of possibility and provided a safe space for us to share how to level up while being ourselves, laughing, crying, and everything in between.

To my mentors, you know who you are. Thank you for always having my back. Thank you for supporting me through my pivots and life and work transitions. You have always believed I could do anything, and there are many times I've had to borrow that belief before I could embody it myself. You have opened doors for me in ways I could have never imagined as a young girl. You have no idea how much your presence, advice, and support have meant to me. I'm forever grateful.

To my clients, it's my honor to be your coach and a part of your lives in such an intimate way. Working with you gives me life and reinforces my purpose on this planet. Know that I will never share the details of your stories; they are sacred treasures.

To my book coach, Stacy Ennis. You were the very first person to hear my ideas for this book. You encouraged me to stay focused on my mission and to keep writing despite all the negative self-talk I battled so often. You kept me on task in the most loving get-it-done, you-can-do-this kind of way. I'm so thankful for you.

To my book editor, Brooke White. From the very beginning, you connected with me and with this book. You understood its purpose and its potential impact. You didn't allow me to get in my own way in the editing process and made my words on these pages truly shine. Thank you for championing me and this book.

To the entire Greenleaf team, thank you for all you've done to shepherd me through the publishing process and to ensure this book reached as many readers as possible. I'm grateful for your support and dedication to this book and its mission.

Last but not least, to my community of Latina and women of color professionals, it's our time. You continue to inspire me and push me to continue fully expressing all that I am. I hope this book makes you proud and emboldens you to be all you are and live your truth.

GET IN TOUCH

To connect with Arivee

 Visit **www.ariveevargas.com** where you'll find more information on her coaching programs, courses, and workshops.

 @ariveevargas

in/ariveevargas/

NOTES

CHAPTER 2

1. Josie Cox, "The perfect storm keeping women of colour behind at work," BBC, posted March 1, 2023, https://www.bbc.com/worklife/article/20230228-the-perfect-storm-keeping-women-of-colour-behind-at-work.

2. Jess Huang, Alexis Krivkovich, Ishanaa Rambachan, and Lareina Yee, "For mothers in the workplace, a year (and counting) like no other," McKinsey & Company, posted May 5, 2021, https://www.mckinsey.com/featured-insights/diversity-and-inclusion/for-mothers-in-the-workplace-a-year-and-counting-like-no-other.

3. A 2015 study in the *Journal of Family Issues* found that Latina mothers reported higher work-family conflict than White mothers, which the authors linked to Latina cultural scripts emphasizing mothers' familial roles; Research reviewed in a 2012 book chapter indicated Asian-American mothers may feel more guilt when utilizing childcare due to cultural values prioritizing maternal care; A 2005 study in the *Journal of Marriage and Family* found African-American mothers experienced greater role overload trying to manage work and family obligations compared to White mothers.

4. Rosa Maria Gil and Carmen Inoa Vazquez, *The Maria Paradox: How Latinas Can Merge Old World Traditions with New World Self-Esteem* (New York City: Open Road Integrated Media, 2014), https://books.google.com/books?hl=en&lr=&id=Lzz6AwAAQBAJ&oi=fnd&pg=PT6&ots=fL6kBloP8b&sig=Rmk_UoSuu5Ok3ia9yYEgx75FFDc#v=onepage&q&f=false; Roberto J. Velasquez, Leticia M. Arellano, and Brian W. McNeill, *The Handbook of Chicana/o Psychology and Mental Health*, Yolanda Flores

Niemann "Stereotypes of Chicanas and Chicanos: Impact on Family Functioning, Individual Expectations, Goals, and Behavior," (New York: Routledge 2004), https://doi.org/10.4324/9781410610911.

CHAPTER 3

1. McKinsey & Company and Lean In, "Women in the Workplace 2023 Report," https://sgff-media.s3.amazonaws.com/sgff_r1eHetbDYb/Women+in+the+Workplace+2023_+Designed+Report.pdf.

2. Catalyst, "Advancing African American Women in the Workplace: What Managers Need to Know" (2004), https://www.catalyst.org/wp-content/uploads/2019/01/Advancing_African_American_Women_in_the_Workplace_What_Managers_Need_to_Know.pdf.

3. S. M. Nkomo and T. Cox, Jr., "Diverse identities in organizations," in *Handbook of Organization Studies* (London: Sage Publications, 1996): 338–356.

4. Zuhairah Washington and Laura Morgan Roberts, "Women of Color Get Less Support at Work. Here's How Managers Can Change That," *Harvard Business Review*, posted March 4, 2019, https://hbr.org/2019/03/women-of-color-get-less-support-at-work-heres-how-managers-can-change-that.

5. Joan C. Williams, Marina Multhaup, Su Li, and Rachel Korn of the Center for Worklife Law at the University of California, Hastings College of the Law, "You Can't Change What You Can't See: Interrupting Racial & Gender Bias in the Legal Profession," conducted jointly with the ABA Commission on Women in the Profession and the Minority Corporate Counsel Association, https://nysba.org/NYSBA/Meetings%20Department/2019%20Annual%20Meeting/Coursebooks/Women%20in%20Law/1%20ABA%20Commission%20on%20Women.pdf.

6. Lean In, "Women in the Workplace 2021," (2021), https://leanin.org/women-in-the-workplace/2021/women-of-color-continue-to-have-a-worse-experience-at-work.

7. Shruti Mukkamala and Karen L. Suyemoto, "Racialized sexism/sexualized racism: A multimethod study of intersectional experiences of discrimination for Asian American women," *Asian American Journal of Psychology* 9, no. 1 (March 2018): 32–46, http://dx.doi.org/10.1037/aap0000104.

8. McKinsey & Company and Lean In, "Women in the Workplace 2023 Report."

9. Catalyst, "Advancing African American Women in the Workplace: What Managers Need to Know." Daphna Motro, Jonathan B. Evans, Aleksander P. J. Ellis, and Lehman Benson III, "The 'Angry Black Woman' Stereotype at Work," *Harvard Business Review*, posted January 31, 2022, https://hbr.org/2022/01/the-angry-black-woman-stereotype-at-work?utm_medium=paidsearch&utm_source=google&utm_campaign=domcontent_bussoc&utm_term=Non-Brand&tpcc=domcontent_bussoc&gad_source=1&gclid=CjwKCAjwrcKxBhBMEiwAIVF8rD6q-pWMRtrQfvRiV9rz_hSTlxEDrJi8q0hgnOkRNabReKC5XHMgHxoC0aEQAvD_BwE.

10. Catalyst, "Advancing African American Women in the Workplace: What Managers Need to Know."

11. Mark Paul, Khaing Zaw, and William Darity, "Returns in the Labor Market: A Nuanced View of Penalties at the Intersection of Race and Gender in the US," *Feminist Economics* 28, no. 2 (March 2022): 1–31, https://www.tandfonline.com/doi/full/10.1080/13545701.2022.2042472?scroll=top&needAccess=true; McKinsey & Company and Lean In, "Women in the Workplace 2023 Report"; Isabela Salas-Betsch, "Ending Discrimination and Harassment at Work," Playbook for the Advancement of Women in the Economy (March 14, 2024), https://www.americanprogress.org/article/playbook-for-the-advancement-of-women-in-the-economy/ending-discrimination-and-harassment-at-work/.

12. Monnica T. Williams, "Microaggressions: Clarification, Evidence, and Impact," *Perspectives on Psychological Science* 15, no. 1 (August 2019), https://journals.sagepub.com/doi/full/10.1177/1745691619827499.

13. Derald Wing Sue, Christina M. Capodilupo, Gina C. Torino, Jennifer M. Bucceri, Aisha M. B. Holder, Kevin L. Nadal, and Marta Esquilin, "Racial microaggressions in everyday life: Implications for clinical practice," *American Psychologist* 62, no. 4 (May 2007): 271–86, https://www.researchgate.net/publication/6315413_Racial_microaggressions_in_everyday_life_Implications_for_clinical_practice.

14. McKinsey & Company and Lean In, "Women in the Workplace 2023 Report."

15. Lean In, "Women in the Workplace 2021."

16. Lean In, "Women in the Workplace 2021."

17. Paula L. Costa, Jessica W. McDuffie, Stephanie E. V. Brown, Yimin He, Brittany N. Ikner, Isaac E. Sabat, and Kathi N. Miner, "Microaggressions: Mega problems or micro issues? A meta-analysis," *Journal of Community Psychology* 51, no. 1

(May 2022), https://doi.org/10.1002/jcop.22885; Colin Harrison and Kimberly D. Tanner, "Language Matters: Considering Microaggressions in Science," *CBE: Life Sciences Education* 17 no. 1 (Spring 2018), https://www.ncbi.nlm.nih.gov/ pmc/articles/PMC6007773/.

18. Derald Wing Sue, Jennifer Bucceri, Annie I. Lin, Kevin L. Nadal, and Gina C. Torino, "Racial Microaggressions and the Asian American Experience," *Cultural Diversity and Ethnic Minority Psychology* 13, no. 1 (2007): 72–81, https://www .apa.org/pi/oema/resources/ethnicity-health/asian-american/microaggressions -asians.pdf.

19. Kevin L. Nadal, Silvia L. Mazzula, David Paul Rivera, and Whitney Fujii-Doe, "Microaggressions and Latina/o Americans: An Analysis of Nativity, Gender, and Ethnicity," *Journal of Latinx Psychology* 2, no. 2 (April 2014): 67.

20. Lucas Torres and Joelle T. Taknint, "Ethnic Microaggressions, Traumatic Stress Symptoms, and Latino Depression: A Moderated Mediational Model," *Journal of Counseling Psychology* 62, no. 3 (July 2015), https://epublications.marquette .edu/cgi/viewcontent.cgi?article=1199&context=psych_fac.

21. Kathy Gurchiek, "Want to Be Inclusive? Learn How to Pronounce Other People's Names," SHRM, posted October 20, 2021, https://www.shrm.org/ topics-tools/news/inclusion-equity-diversity/want-to-inclusive-learn-how-to -pronounce-peoples-names.

22. Naomi Torres-Mackie, "Understanding Name-Based Microaggressions," *Psychology Today*, posted September 29, 2019, https://www.psychologytoday .com/us/blog/underdog-psychology/201909/understanding-name-based -microaggressions; Kathy Gurchiek, "Want to Be Inclusive? Learn How to Pronounce Other People's Names."

23. McKinsey & Company and Lean In, "Women in the Workplace 2023 Report."

24. McKinsey & Company and Lean In, "Women in the Workplace 2023 Report."

25. McKinsey & Company and Lean In, "Women in the Workplace 2022 Report," https://wiw-report.s3.amazonaws.com/Women_in_the_Workplace_2022.pdf.

26. McKinsey & Company and Lean In, "Women in the Workplace 2022 Report."

27. Dan Witters and Sangeeta Agrawal, "The Economic Cost of Poor Employee Mental Health" Gallup, updated December 13, 2022, https://www.gallup.com/ workplace/404174/economic-cost-poor-employee-mental-health.aspx.

28. Witters and Agrawal, "The Economic Cost of Poor Employee Mental Health."

CHAPTER 4

1. Cleveland Clinic Staff, "Got Mom Guilt? Here's How to Navigate It," Cleveland Clinic, posted April 28, 2023, https://health.clevelandclinic.org/mom-guilt.

2. Lianne Aarntzen, Belle Derks, Elianne van Steenbergen, Michelle Ryan, and Tanja van der Lippe, "Work-family guilt as a straightjacket [sic]. An interview and diary study on consequences of mothers' work-family guilt," *Journal of Vocational Behavior* 115 (December 2019): 103336, https://pure.rug.nl/ws/portalfiles/portal/226930753/1_s2.0_S0001879119301083_main.pdf.

3. Raquel Sánchez-Rodríguez, Émilie Orsini, Elodie Laflaquière, Stacey Callahan, and Natalène Séjourné, "Depression, anxiety, and guilt in mothers with burnout of preschool and school-aged children: Insight from a cluster analysis," *Journal of Affective Disorders* 259, no. 6 (August 2019), https://doi.org/10.1016/j.jad.2019.08.031; Aarntzen, Derks, van Steenbergen, Ryan, and Lippe, "Work-family guilt."

4. Peter Thomas Sandy, Tebogo K. Molotsi, and Margaret Rioga, "Work-Family Conflict and Mental Distress of Black Women in Employment in South Africa: A Template Analysis," *Social Sciences* 11, no. 9 (August 2022): 382, https://www.mdpi.com/2076-0760/11/9/382#B13-socsci-11-00382.

5. Melody Montano, Lauren Mizock, and Esther Calzada, "The Maternal Guilt of Working Latina Mothers: A Qualitative Study," *Hispanic Journal of Behavioral Sciences* 45, no. 3 (April 5, 2023): 149–171, https://doi.org/10.1177/07399863241239991.

6. Montano, Mizock, and Calzada, "The Maternal Guilt of Working Latina Mothers."

7. Montano, Mizock, and Calzada, "The Maternal Guilt of Working Latina Mothers."

8. Brené Brown, *Atlas of the Heart: Mapping Meaningful Connection and the Language of Human Experience* (New York: Random House, 2021), 214.

9. Michael E. McCullough, Robert A. Emmons, and Jo-Ann Tsang, "The grateful disposition: A conceptual and empirical topography," *Journal of Personality and Social Psychology* 82, no. 1 (February 2002): 112–127, https://doi.org/10.1037/0022-3514.82.1.112; Julia K. Boehm, Sonja Lyubomirsky, and Kennon M. Sheldon, "A longitudinal experimental study comparing the effectiveness of happiness-enhancing strategies in Anglo Americans and Asian Americans," *Cognition & Emotion* 25, no. 7 (February 2011): 1263–1272, https://

www.tandfonline.com/doi/full/10.1080/02699931.2010.541227; Robert A. Emmons and Michael E. McCullough, "Counting Blessings Versus Burdens: An Experimental Investigation of Gratitude and Subjective Well-Being in Daily Life," *Journal of Personality and Social Psychology* 84, no. 2 (2003): 377–389, https://greatergood.berkeley.edu/pdfs/GratitudePDFs/6Emmons -BlessingsBurdens.pdf; Robert A. Emmons and Anjali Mishra, "Why Gratitude Enhances Well-Being: What We Know, What We Need to Know," *Designing Positive Psychology: Taking Stock and Moving Forward* (January 2011): 248- 262, https://doi.org/10.1093/acprof:oso/9780195373585.003.0016; Courtney E. Ackerman, "Benefits of Gratitude: 28+ Surprising Research Findings," Positive Psychology, posted April 12, 2017, https://positivepsychology.com/ benefits-gratitude-research-questions//.

CHAPTER 5

1. Dan P. McAdams and William L. Dunlop, *The Person: A New Introduction to Personality Psychology*, 6th ed., (Hoboken: Wiley, 2022).

2. J. C. Williams and J. L. Berdhal, "Work-family conflict and the experiences of women of color," *Journal of Family Theory & Review* 13 (March 2021): 50–65; C. A. Ogunbode and A. G. Ajayi, "Work-family conflict and job satisfaction among women of color in the United States," *Journal of Family and Economic Issues* 42, no. 2 (June 2021): 1890-201; L. A. Winker and R. M. Kanter, "Work-family conflict and the career advancement of women of color," *Journal of Applied Psychology* 105, no. 12 (2020): 1386–1397; B. C. Koford and J. B. Whiting, "Work-family conflict and the mental health of working women of color," *Journal of Social and Personal Relationships* 36, no. 6 (June 2019): 1883–1900.

3. Koford and Whiting, "Work-family conflict and the mental health of working women of color."

CHAPTER 6

1. Paul J. Meyer developed the wheel of life more than sixty years ago. The circle resembles the spokes of a wheel and is used to present the most important areas of your life. There aren't a set number of categories to place on the wheel and the categories listed (i.e., career, finances, family) can be described in various ways. Jeremy Sutton, "How to Apply the Wheel of Life in Coaching,"

Positive Psychology, posted July 29, 2020, https://positivepsychology.com/wheel-of-life-coaching/.

2. Jette Ammentorp, Lisbeth Uhrenfeldt, Flemming Angel, Martin Ehrensvärd, Ebbe Carlsen, and Poul-Erik Kofoed, "Can life coaching improve health outcomes? A systematic review of intervention studies," *BMC Health Services Research* 13, no. 1 (2013): 428-439, https://doi.org/10.1186/1472-6963-13 -428; Una Byrne, "Wheel of Life: Effective steps for stress management," *Business Information Review* 22, no. 2 (June 2005): 123-130, https://doi .org/10.1177/026638210505477.

CHAPTER 7

1. P. L. Hill, N. A. Turiano, D. K. Mroczek, and A. L. Burrow. "The value of purpose in life across adulthood: Age-related patterns and potential mechanisms," *Journal of Personality* 88, no. 3 (June 2020): 423–437; P. L. Hill and N. A. Turiano, "Purpose in life as a predictor of mortality across adulthood," *Psychological Science* 25, no. 7 (May 8, 2014), https://doi.org/10.1177/ 09567976145317; Y. Kuzucu and Y. Ozbay, "The effect of purpose in life on mental health: A meta-analysis," *Journal of Happiness Studies* 21, no. 1 (January 2020): 71–94; Frank Martela and Michael F. Steger, "The three meanings of meaning in life: Distinguishing coherence, purpose, and significance," *The Journal of Positive Psychology* 11, no. 5 (January 2016): 531–545, https://doi.org/10.1080/ 17439760.2015.1137623.

2. "The Future of Jobs Report 2018," World Economic Forum, accessed April 16, 2024, https://www3.weforum.org/docs/WEF_Future_of_Jobs_2018.pdf.

3. Shawn Achor, Andrew Reece, Gabriella Rosen Kellerman, and Alexi Robichaux, "9 Out of 10 People Are Willing to Earn Less Money to Do More-Meaningful Work," *Harvard Business Review*, posted November 6, 2018, https://hbr.org/ 2018/11/9-out-of-10-people-are-willing-to-earn-less-money-to-do-more -meaningful-work.

4. Kim Parker and Rachel Minkin, "What makes for a fulfilling life?" Pew Research Center, posted September 14, 2023, https://www.pewresearch.org/ social-trends/2023/09/14/what-makes-for-a-fulfilling-life/.

5. Theresa Frank and Davina Banner-Lukaris, "The Benefits of Knowing and Caring about Oneself: The Role of Self-Insight and Self-Compassion in Identity and Well-Being," University of Northern British Columbia (November 2021), https://www.doi.org/10.24124/2021/59221; Kristin Neff, "Self-Compassion:

An Alternative Conceptualization of a Healthy Attitude Toward Oneself," *Self and Identity* 2, no. 2 (April 2003): 85–101, https://doi.org/10.1080/ 15298860309032; Letty Y.-Y. Kwan, Yu Sheng Hung, and Lam Lam, "How Can We Reap Learning Benefits for Individuals With Growth and Fixed Mindsets?: Understanding Self-Reflection and Self-Compassion as the Psychological Pathways to Maximize Positive Learning Outcomes," *Frontiers in Education* 7 (April 27, 2022), https://doi.org/10.3389/feduc.2022.800530.

6. Agnieszka Bojanowska and Beata Urbańska, "Individual values and well-being: The moderating role of personality traits," *International Journal of Psychology* 56, no. 5 (October 2021): 698–709, https://doi.org/10.1002/ijop.12751; Paul H. P. Hanel, Hamdullah Tunç, Divija Bhasin, Lukas F. Litzellachner, and Gregory R. Maio, "Value fulfillment and well-being: Clarifying directions over time," *Journal of Personality* (July 27, 2023): 1–13, https://doi.org/10.1111/jopy.12869.

7. Paul Atkins, Alison Christie, and James Donald, "The Meaning and Doing Mindfulness: The Role of Values in the Link Between Mindfulness and Well-being," *Mindfulness* 8 (September 19, 2016): 368–378, https://link.springer.com/article/10.1007/s12671-016-0606-9; Simon Grégoire, Marina Doucerain, Laurence Morin, and Lucy Finkelstein-Fox, "The relationship between value -based actions, psychological distress and well-being: A multilevel diary study," *Journal of Contextual Behavioral Science* 20 (April 2021): 79–88, https://doi .org/10.1016/j.jcbs.2021.03.006.

8. Natasha K. Lekes, "Self-growth, close relationships, and community contribution: Exploring the development of intrinsic value priorities and their influence on well-being," McGill University (2012), https://escholarship.mcgill .ca/concern/theses/3197xq487; Tim Kasser and Richard M. Ryan, "Further examining the American dream: Differential correlates of intrinsic and extrinsic goals," *Personality and Social Psychology Bulletin* 22, no. 3 (March 1996): 280–287, https://doi.org/10.1177/0146167296223006; Tim Kasser and Richard M. Ryan, "A dark side of the American dream: Correlates of financial success as a central life aspiration," *Journal of Personality and Social Psychology* 65, no. 2 (August 1993): 410–422, https://doi.org/10.1037/0022-3514.65.2.410; Tim Kasser, Richard M. Ryan, Charles E. Couchman, and Kennon M. Sheldon, "Materialistic values: Their causes and consequences," T. Kasser and A. D. Kanner (Eds.), *Psychology and consumer culture: The struggle for a good life in a materialistic world* (January 2004): 11–28, https://doi.org/10.1037/10658-002.

9. Lekes, "Self-Growth"; Kasser and Ryan, "Further examining the American dream"; Kasser and Ryan, "A dark side of the American dream"; Kasser and Ryan, "Materialistic values."

10. Florencia M. Sortheix and Shalom H. Schwartz, "Values that underlie and undermine well-being: Variability across countries," *European Journal of Personality* 31, no. 2 (March 1, 2017): 187–201, https://doi.org/10.1002/per.2096; Michael P. Grosz, Shalom H. Schwartz, and Clemens M. Lechner, "The longitudinal interplay between personal values and subjective well-being: A registered report," *European Journal of Personality* 35, no. 6 (May 14, 2021): 881–897, https://doi.org/10.1177/08902070211012923.

11. Lilach Sagiv, Sonia Roccas, Jan Cieciuch, and Shalom H. Schwartz, "Personal values in human life," *Nature Human Behaviour* 1 (August 21, 2017): 630–639, https://doi.org/10.1038/s41562-017-0185-3.

12. M. F. Steger, S. Oishi, and T. B. Kashdan, "Meaning in life across the life span: Levels and correlates of meaning in life from emerging adulthood to older adulthood," *The Journal of Positive Psychology* 4, no. 3 (2009): 209–222, https://doi.org/10.1080/17439760802303127.

13. Martin E. P. Seligman, *Flourish: A Visionary New Understanding of Happiness and Well-being* (New York: Atria Books, 2012), 24.

CHAPTER 8

1. D. J. Hallford, D. W. Austin, K. Takano, and F. Raes, "Psychopathology and episodic future thinking: A systematic review and meta-analysis of specificity and episodic detail," *Behavior Research and Therapy* 102, (March 2018): 42–51, https://doi.org/10.1016/j.brat.2018.01.003.

2. F. Craik and R. Lockhart, "Levels of Processing: A Framework for Memory Research," *Journal of Verbal Learning and Behavior* 11, no. 6 (December 1972): 671–684, http://mrbartonmaths.com/resourcesnew/8. Research/Memory and Revision/Levels of Processing.pdf.

3. Pam A. Mueller and Daniel M. Oppenheimer, "The pen is mightier than the keyboard: Advantages of longhand over laptop note taking," *Psychological Science* 25, no. 6 (June 2014): 1159–68, https://doi.org/10.1177/0956797614524581.

4. Mueller and Oppenheimer, "The pen is mightier than the keyboard."

5. Julie Delose and Michelle vanDellen, "The role of temporal distance on forecasting the difficulty of goal pursuits," *The Journal of Social Psychology* 163, no. 25 (January 2022): 1–20, https://doi.org/10.1080/00224545.2021.2020204.

CHAPTER 10

1. Darren T. Baker and Juliet Bourke, "How Confidence Is Weaponized Against Women," *Harvard Business Review*, posted October 20, 2022, https://hbr .org/2022/10/how-confidence-is-weaponized-against-women.

2. Diana Aline Nôga, Elisa de Mello E. Souza Meth, André Pekkola Pacheco, Xiao Tan, Jonathan Cedernaes, Lieve Thecla van Egmond, Pei Xue, and Christian Benedict, "Habitual short sleep duration, diet, and development of type 2 diabetes in adults," *JAMA Network Open* 7, no. 3 (March 5, 2024): 241147, http:// doi:10.1001/jamanetworkopen.2024.1147; Rebecca C. Thurston, Yuefang Chang, Christopher E. Kline, Leslie M. Swanson, Samar R. El Khoudary, Elizabeth A. Jackson, and Carol A. Derby, "Trajectories of Sleep Over Midlife and Incident Cardiovascular Disease Events in the Study of Women's Health Across the Nation," *Circulation* 149, no. 7 (February 13, 2024), https://doi .org/10.1161/CIRCULATIONAHA.123.066491; Sanjay R. Patel, Atul Malhotra, David P. White, Daniel J. Gottlieb, and Frank B. Hu, "Association between reduced sleep and weight gain in women," *American Journal of Epidemiology* 164, no. 10 (December 2006): 947–54, https://doi.org/10.1093/aje/ kwj280.

CHAPTER 11

1. Robert Waldinger and Marc Schulz, *The Good Life: Lessons from the World's Longest Scientific Study of Happiness* (New York: Simon & Schuster, 2023).

2. Waldinger and Schulz, *The Good Life*.

3. Shimon Saphire-Bernstein and Shelley E. Taylor, "Close Relationships and Happiness," *The Oxford Handbook of Happiness* (August 1, 2013): 821–833, https://doi.org/10.1093/oxfordhb/9780199557257.013.0060; Jared R. McShall and Matthew D. Johnson, "The Association Between Relationship Quality and Physical Health Across Racial and Ethnic Groups," *Journal of Cross-Cultural Psychology* 46, no. 6 (June 8, 2015): 789-804, https://doi.org/10.1177/ 0022022115587026; Melikşah Demir, Metin Özdemir, and Lesley A.

Weitekamp, "Looking to Happy Tomorrows with Friends: Best and Close Friendships as they Predict Happiness," *Journal of Happiness Studies* 8, no. 2, (February 2007): 243–271, https://doi.org/10.1007/s10902-006-9025-2.

4. Hakan Ozcelik and Sigal Barsade, "Work loneliness and employee performance," *Academy of Management Proceedings* (January 2011): 1-6, https://faculty .wharton.upenn.edu/wp-content/uploads/2012/05/Work_Loneliness_ Performance_Study.pdf.

5. GWL Team, "60 Percent of Female Executives Feel Lonelier as their Careers Progress finds Survey," *Global Woman Leader*, posted March 14, 2023, https:// www.theglobalwomanleader.com/viewpoint/experts-column/60-percent-of -female-executives-feellonelier-as-their-careers-progress-finds-survey-nwid -267.html#:~:text=.

6. GWL Team, "60 Percent of Female Executives Feel Lonelier as their Careers Progress finds Survey."

7. Megan Leonhardt, "More American women are single than ever before— and it's costing them big money," Yahoo! Finance, updated March 18, 2023, https://finance.yahoo.com/news/more-american-women-single-ever-130000779 .html?guccounter=1&guce_referrer=aHR0cHM6Ly93d3cuZ29vZ2xl mNvbS8&guce_referrer_sig=AQAAALtPY60b-V8sP6zP007bbyrP -KyVFx0GyNFpEBG5NT0Ywk9JkAaAkG2Z2FuvIIIBQ6ZSOqgSM2 -XNuHNnNYSTAAu-eQU-NdDMKstwXPBZvrGIRNn-gnsUh67vSa05J6_ G7_HA58u3jTVs5oY8jTAG7aVZcYdzH27HMQUfxiTj4r8.

8. Daniel A. Cox, "The State of American Friendship: Change, Challenges, and Loss: Findings from the May 2021 American Perspectives Survey," Survey Center on American Life, posted June 8, 2021, https://www.americansurvey center.org/research/the-state-of-american-friendship-change-challenges -and-loss/.

9. Richard Fry, Carolina Aragão, Kiley Hurst, and Kim Parker, "In a Growing Share of U.S. Marriages, Husbands and Wives Earn About the Same," Pew Research Center, posted April 13, 2023, https://www.pewresearch.org/social -trends/2023/04/13/in-a-growing-share-of-u-s-marriages-husbands-and-wives -earn-about-the-same/.

10. Sarah Jane Glynn, "An Unequal Division of Labor: How Equitable Workplace Policies Would Benefit Working Mothers," CAP 20, posted May 18, 2018, https://www.americanprogress.org/article/unequal-division-labor/.

11. Kei Nomaguchi and Melissa A. Milkie, "Parenthood and Well-Being: A Decade in Review," *Journal of Marriage and Family* 82, no. 1 (January 5, 2020): 198–223, https://doi.org/10.1111/jomf.12646.

12. Nomaguchi and Milkie, "Parenthood and Well-Being."

13. K. E. Cavanaugh and R. L. Huston, "Work-family conflict and the well-being of women of color: The role of social support," *Journal of Career Development* 47, no. 6 (2020): 631–646; D. Kim and J. Kim, "Work-family conflict and job satisfaction: The moderating role of job control and social support," *Journal of Vocational Behavior* 119 (2020): 1034.

ABOUT THE AUTHOR

Arivee N. Vargas is the host of the *Humble Rising* podcast, a certified executive coach, writer, speaker, and mother of three.

She's the founder and CEO of Humble Rising LLC, which aims to empower women to stand in their truth, worth, and power to create a life and career they want and deserve, with joy, fulfillment, and aliveness. Arivee's work centers on helping women professionals, and first-generation and women of color in particular, navigate personal and professional inflection points to move forward with clarity, confidence, and inner alignment.

In her previous life, Arivee was a litigator at two large law firms, in-house lawyer, and corporate compliance leader. She was also a people and organizational development leader, focusing on leadership development for current and emerging senior leaders, and served as a lecturer at Boston College's Carroll School of Management for several years. Arivee has been named one of top executive coaches in Boston for the past three years, and has been the recipient of numerous awards and recognitions over the course of her career including receiving an honorary degree from

Boston College in 2022, being named as one of Boston Business Journal's 40 under 40, and one of *Hispanic Executive* magazine's featured Latina Leaders in the biotech industry. Arivee's work has been featured in *Oprah Daily*, *Forbes*, *Success Magazine*, *Hispanic Executive* magazine, *Authority Magazine*, the *Boston Business Journal*, FIERCE by Mitú, YourTango, Thrive Global, BizWomen, the Mother Chapter, and more. Arivee is a proud alumna of Boston College and Boston College Law School.